Michel Foucault

AF837963

This book explores the theoretical contribution of Michel Foucault to the fields of criminology, law, justice and penology. It surveys both the ways in which the work of Foucault has been applied in criminology, but also how his work can be used to understand and explain contemporary issues and policies. Moreover, this book seeks to dispel some of the common misconceptions about the relevance of Foucault's work to criminology and law.

Mariana Valverde clearly explains the insights that Foucault's rich body of work provides about different practices found in the fields of law, security, justice and punishment; and how these insights have been used or could be used to understand and explain issues and policies that Foucault himself did not write about, including those that had not yet emerged during his lifetime.

Drawing on key texts by Foucault such as *Discipline and Punish*, and also lectures he gave at the Collège de France and Louvain Criminology Institute, which offer a more nuanced account of the development of criminal justice, Mariana Valverde offers the essential text on Foucault and his contribution and continued relevance to criminology. This book will be important reading for students and scholars of criminology, law, sociolegal studies, security studies, political theory and sociological theory.

Mariana Valverde is Professor of Criminology at the University of Toronto. She is the author of *Chronotopes of Law: Jurisdiction, Scale and Governance* (Routledge, 2015) and *Law and Order: Images, Meanings, Myths* (Routledge, 2006).

Routledge Key Thinkers in Criminology

Edited by Tom Daems, University of Leuven
Kelly Hannah-Moffat, University of Toronto Mississauga
Shadd Maruna, University of Manchester
Tim Newburn, London School of Economics and Political Science

The more a discipline matures and develops the more interesting it becomes to document and reflect upon its history – including its key figures. The history of criminology includes a set of key thinkers who have defined the subject, renewed its theory and refined its methodology.

The volumes in this series are stand-alone introductions and critical examinations of the life and work of key thinkers in criminology. These volumes collectively contribute to writing and rewriting criminology's history by adding a distinctive line of inquiry: the focus on the ideas of some of the most inspiring figures from its past.

1. Michel Foucault
Mariana Valverde

Michel Foucault

Mariana Valverde

Routledge
Taylor & Francis Group
LONDON AND NEW YORK

First published 2017 by Routledge

2 Park Square, Milton Park, Abingdon, Oxfordshire OX14 4RN
52 Vanderbilt Avenue, New York, NY 10017

Routledge is an imprint of the Taylor & Francis Group, an informa business

First issued in paperback 2019

Copyright © 2017 Mariana Valverde

The right of Mariana Valverde to be identified as author of this work has been asserted by her in accordance with sections 77 and 78 of the Copyright, Designs and Patents Act 1988.

All rights reserved. No part of this book may be reprinted or reproduced or utilised in any form or by any electronic, mechanical, or other means, now known or hereafter invented, including photocopying and recording, or in any information storage or retrieval system, without permission in writing from the publishers.

Notice:
Product or corporate names may be trademarks or registered trademarks, and are used only for identification and explanation without intent to infringe.

British Library Cataloguing in Publication Data
A catalogue record for this book is available from the British Library

Library of Congress Cataloging in Publication Data
Names: Valverde, Mariana, 1955- author.
Title: Michel Foucault / Mariana Valverde.
Description: Abingdon, Oxon ; New York, NY : Routledge, 2017. | Series:
Routledge key thinkers in criminology | Includes bibliographical references and index.
Identifiers: LCCN 2016041911| ISBN 9781138657083 (hardback) | ISBN 9781315621517 (ebook)
Subjects: LCSH: Criminology–Philosophy. | Criminal justice, Administration of–Philosophy. | Foucault, Michel, 1926-1984.
Classification: LCC HV6018 .V35 2017 | DDC 364.01–dc23
LC record available at https://lccn.loc.gov/2016041911

ISBN: 978-1-138-65708-3 (hbk)
ISBN: 978-0-367-22654-1 (pbk)

Typeset in Goudy
by Taylor & Francis Books

Contents

Table

Acknowledgements

Reading and reflecting on theoretically innovative work, such as Michel Foucault's publications and lectures, may appear at first sight a solitary activity. But in fact theoretical work (just like empirical research) is rooted in dialogical relationships, conducted both in person and via writings and publications. Given that many of the dialogical relationships that have been important for me and for this book stretch back over a 25-year period, it would be impossible to list here all the people and the groups and institutions that have contributed directly or indirectly to this book. I can only name a few: the Toronto History of the Present research group (which flourished in the 1990s); Mitchell Dean, Kelly Hannah Moffat, Bernard Harcourt, Engin Isin, Paula Maurutto, Pat O'Malley, Nikolas Rose and William Walters. I also need to thank the successive cohorts of University of Toronto students whose questions and insights greatly helped me to develop ways of explaining Foucault's work and showing how it might be used today. I owe particular gratitude to the brave undergraduates who in 2015 asked me to run a special reading course on Foucault's work: Andreas Aaravositas, Jack Galligan, Vincent Harinam, Yael Kogan and Amy Lin. Leading that largely self-taught seminar-style course was a great pleasure, and helped me a great deal in planning this book.

Chapter 1

Preliminaries: Foucault's search for a place from which to challenge academic disciplines

Typing 'Marx and criminology' into Google Scholar, you get 17,200 hits. Moving into the twentieth century, Erving Goffman's contribution to criminology is a topic in 5,210 articles and books. 'Michel Foucault and criminology', by contrast, gets 25,400 hits. This is not the largest piece of the current scholarly criminology pie ('feminism and criminology', for example, collectively earns 29,000 hits); but, given that theory of any sort is a minority interest, the number of hits in Google Scholar for Foucault and criminology is one indication that his work is being used and cited by criminologists with great frequency. This is especially true in the English-speaking world outside the US; but even in the somewhat hostile arena of US criminology Foucault's name is as well known as that of any theorist.

The prominence of Foucault's name in the academic field of criminology would not be surprising if Foucault had decided to use his considerable research capacities and literary skills, together with his original mind and privileged position in the international academy, to become a famous criminologist. But Foucault never had any institutional or intellectual association with criminology; and, perhaps surprisingly, the unusually large collection of fields in which he did a great deal of reading and/or original research did not include either sociology or criminal law (although, as we shall see in Chapter 7, Foucault did research and analyse aspects of the history of criminal procedure). What is more, Foucault sometimes went out of his way to denounce criminology as such. These comments, mainly expressed in interviews rather than in a properly researched book, should be taken with a grain of salt. One factor to consider is that France did not experience the same 'boom' in critical left-wing criminology as Britain, Italy, and other countries did during the 1970s, and so Foucault had a limited understanding of the breadth and diversity of criminological research. But nevertheless the comments that have been published do not exactly presage a great future as a criminological star:

> Question. You are very hard on criminology, its 'garrulous discourse', its 'endless repetitions'.
>
> Answer. Have you ever read any criminological texts? They are staggering. And I say this out of astonishment, not aggressiveness, because I fail to comprehend how the discourse of criminology has been able to go on at this level. One has the impression that it is of such utility ... for the working of the system, that it does not even need to seek a theoretical justification for itself, or even simply a coherent framework ... I think one needs to investigate why such a 'learned' discourse became so indispensable to the functioning of the nineteenth-century penal system ... Once you suppress the idea of vengeance, which previously was the act of a sovereign threatened in his very sovereignty by the crime, punishment can only have a meaning within a technology of reform [and rehabilitation].
>
> Question. In short, criminological discourse is only useful for giving judges a semblance of a good conscience?
>
> Answer. Yes: or rather it is indispensable in enabling them to judge.
>
> (Foucault 1975: 47–8)

So if Foucault did not see himself as contributing to criminology, even from the outside, what was his position in the academy? How did he find or create a place for himself from which to launch attacks on criminology?

The answer to this question is not straightforward. Attacks on methodologies or whole disciplines are generally launched from the standpoint of a rival discipline or methodology. Historians, for example, constantly complain about sociologists' presentist analyses of this or that problem, while sociologists critique psychological explanations of behaviour for being overly individualist. And in France, where philosophy is taught in a serious manner at high school level, it is certainly common for empirical and policy studies of all kinds to be either critiqued or, more often, wholly ignored by those who assume that philosophy is the queen of the sciences.

It would be rash to claim that Foucault was somehow able to individually rise wholly above the predictable critiques that are continually generated by denouncing one scholarly enterprise from the standpoint of a different one. It is not clear that anyone who works in and succeeds in today's academy can claim to live and work in some kind of post-disciplinary, neutral space. For most of his career Michel Foucault had the great privilege of holding a chair at the Collège de France, a non-teaching institution where the select few simply give lectures to the public on their own research, whatever that may be, rather than having to fit their teaching into established programmes and departments, as the vast majority of university instructors do. That exalted position gave Foucault an intellectual freedom unknown to professors in normal universities, even those who hold explicitly interdisciplinary positions. In early modern Europe someone like John Locke or René Descartes could authoritatively write books on any topic of their choosing; educated gentlemen were not only allowed but also encouraged to range across all types of knowledge, from experimental science to mathematics to philosophy to what later became political science. Ever since the disciplinarization of universities that took place around a century ago, however, a process linked to the marked decline of non-university based scholarship in the period after World War II, developing non-disciplinary or post-disciplinary methods and approaches has become about as difficult as successfully creating a new language.

In our increasingly disciplined scholarly world, in which scholars who are not employed in universities to serve particular teaching needs are few and far between, and learning in general is increasingly 'departmentalized', Foucault tried very hard to not take any one established discipline or standpoint for granted. To do so, he did not take up any kind of super-philosophical position above the fray; that kind of claim would have gone quite against the grain of the Nietzsche-inspired view that all quests for knowledge including scholarly endeavours are situated and contextual. What he did is all that one can do in our own day, namely, use one established knowledge after another, more often than not implicitly rather than explicitly. History was about the only discipline for which Foucault showed respect in his writings, although few historians believe that he took their methodologies seriously – a noted exception to the general dismissal of Foucault by historians is Paul Veyne (2010). Overall, in the interests of appreciating the institutional and material conditions of scholarly thought, it needs to be stressed that Foucault enjoyed an amazing intellectual freedom, in part due to his early decision to avoid the academy in favour of cultural foreign service work, and in part due to his luck in later obtaining one of the very scarce Collège de France chairs at a time in life when, unlike many of his colleagues, he was still young enough to really take real advantage of that opportunity (Macey 1993).

In my view, Foucault's effort to rely as little as possible on the established paradigms of any of the disciplines and epistemologies available to him is paradoxically what unifies a career that was marked by a diversity bordering on eclecticism. 'Diversity' here does not refer only to the very different topics researched by Foucault: eighteenth-century grammar; Renaissance ideas of 'folly' as a normal part of the human condition; nineteenth-century public health; Greco-Roman ethics; the writings of pre-medieval Church Fathers; early psychiatric writings on sexuality; Blanchot's avant-garde literary experiments; twentieth-century liberal political economy; and of course Kant, Nietzsche, Freud, and a long etcetera. What I am here calling 'diversity', and which could just as well be called heterogeneity or even inconsistency, extends to his writing style. The fact that Foucault's writing style changed very markedly over the years is rarely discussed in the numerous works that summarize and explain Foucault; but, in my opinion, the issue is important.

More than any of the few overt methodological statements, the quite abrupt changes in writing style mark, in my view,

Foucault's constant and passionate effort to push in different directions rather than remain content with churning out more work using the same intellectual meat grinder, as academics generally do. An early work such as *Les mots et les choses* (*The Order of Things*, 1970) – which presents a highly original account of the emergence of 'the human sciences' at a time before sociology, psychology, and even biology were academic disciplines – is very difficult to read even for someone like myself, who studied European intellectual history for both my MA and my PhD and is thus familiar with many of the authors and topics covered there. That early book does feature strikingly vivid concrete images instead of chapter introductions, a rhetorical choice perfected in later books; but those opening scenes are then explained in a rather turgid and often highly abstract prose that reminds one of the worst excesses of philosophers like Foucault's early mentor, Louis Althusser, even though the content of the book is on the whole anti-philosophical.

Some years later, *Discipline and Punish* (1977) abandoned the previous high-theory style, and indeed departed markedly from all of the established conventions for writing theoretical books – while also carefully eschewing the conventions of historical scholarship, which would normally be the alternative for someone who wanted to write about how modern prisons came into being and became popular despite their evident failure to reform inmates. *Discipline and Punish* contains some of the most vivid, concrete descriptions of penal practices that have ever been penned by a scholar; indeed, there are passages in this book that would not be unsuitable as a starting vignette for a gripping Hollywood film. But historians, who as a group love a good story, don't like the book because it selects events and penal reforms for extended discussion that were not necessarily representative, and it rides roughshod over conventional periodizations. The book covers the period of the French Revolution, for example, but hardly mentions it – an omission that implicitly makes the important and at that time novel point that changes in political systems and in legislation may not be as important as front-line practices of punishment; but that makes the book look truly peculiar to the average historian. To give an analogy, if Foucault had written about slavery in the US, it is quite possible he might have done so without talking about the Civil War – and, what is more, without ever explaining, even in methodological footnotes, why he made the choices he made.

The last books that Foucault published during his lifetime – *The Use of Pleasure* and *The Care of the Self* (volumes 2 and 3 of *The History of Sexuality* 1984 and 1988) – present an even starker contrast with Foucault's purposively dense and abstract prose of the 1960s. They use everyday language almost exclusively, and are mainly descriptive rather than theoretical. In these very slim volumes, written in a remarkably low-key style, Foucault reads minor Greek and Roman texts that give advice on daily life ethics – from regulating one's eating and drinking, to ensuring that as one gains power and prestige one still has friends to keep one honest, to making a habit of evaluating one's actions on a daily basis. The little books subtly suggest, without any flag-waving or any memorable theoretical claims, that adapting these methods for governing oneself for modern use might offer a healthy alternative to the heavy-duty scrutiny of the self that is recommended and practised by both Christianity and psychoanalysis. But theory as we know it is absent. Indeed, if the words 'Michel Foucault' had not been visible on the covers, few readers would have guessed that they were the product of the same pen that gave us the book that made him famous, *The Order of Things*, the 1970 work that was a best-seller in France; though, as Foucault's biographer says, it's doubtful that many of the people who bought it actually read it all the way through (Macey 1993: 172).

Having argued that the very marked and unusual shifts in writing style that one finds in Foucault's work indicate a constant quest to experiment with ways of going beyond established disciplines (especially philosophy), what can we then conclude about Foucault's standpoint and methodological inclinations? Or, more modestly, what important points about Foucault's intellectual resources need to be made here, in a book aimed at criminology and legal studies students?

In his youth, after immersing himself in European philosophy as was expected of every French scholar outside of the natural sciences, Foucault decided to study psychology and the history of science. He first made a name for himself with books arising from two related lines of inquiry: the historical medicalization of madness and the emergence of confinement as the default solution (*The Birth of the Clinic* 1973; *Madness and Civilization* 1965).

It was only relatively late in life, when he was already a well-established scholar, that Foucault erupted into criminology – or, more accurately, that he saw his work being faithfully read and heavily used by criminologists, in the mid-1980s. This sudden eruption was the result of the great popularity of the book *Discipline and Punish*, issued in French in 1975 and in English in 1977. A useful marker of Foucault's canonization among criminologists is the fact that David Garland, possibly the most influential criminological theorist of our time, devoted two chapters of his 1990 magnum opus *Punishment and Modern Society* to Foucault – the same treatment given to Durkheim and to the Marxist tradition.

Foucault's star rose even higher in the early 1990s, as his posthumously published work on 'governmentality' was adapted for use by researchers working on security, risk management, crime control, and regulation. Even as the insights into modern forms of power and control borrowed from *Discipline and Punish* continued to yield criminological fruit, the posthumously published work on 'government' and 'security' proved extremely useful to progressive criminologists (as will be discussed in Chapters 4 and 5). Tired of railing against 'the state' (as was routinely done in the 1970s), many critical criminologists began to distance themselves from Marxist generalities in the late 1980s and early 1990s, and instead turned their attention to empirically documenting mechanisms of control that cross the state–civil society boundary. Empirical research on private security, on bureaucracies of social assistance, on youth programmes and women's 'empowerment', on 'life skills' training for inmates, and so on was plentiful. And these researchers were looking for new ideas, given that the notion of 'social control', brought in to social science to underline those features of social power that civil society and familial institutions share with coercive state power, had come to be seen as over-inclusive, top-down, and lacking in precision (Melossi 1990; Rose et al. 2006).

There is by now a vast literature evaluating what Foucault's work contributes or can contribute to contemporary studies of crime prevention, risk management, punishment, and security writ large. But the criminologists who argue amongst themselves about Foucault's contribution tend to take the concerns and questions privileged by criminology for granted, and hence limit themselves to discussing whether X or Y idea from Foucault's work furthers or does not further the criminological project (as indeed Garland does in his celebrated *Punishment and Modern Society* 1990). Throughout this book, I will turn the discussion in a different direction to argue that Foucault's most significant legacy is not so much a set of explanations or concepts that address existing questions, but rather his approach, his style of thought – an approach that quietly, unpolemically, sidelines the traditional critical questions about who has the power and who benefits from this or that situation that critical legal studies, Marxist criminology, and feminist social science put at the centre of their inquiries. (For more on this see Valverde 2010.)

Foucault's quest to go beyond structuralism

Foucault's aim was not to reveal the hidden structures of power: the Marxists of his day, who in the 1960s and 1970s dominated the critical academy in Paris as in most of the world, had done that very well already, and would continue to do so for all of Foucault's lifetime. (In fact, Foucault's death in 1984 came at the time when Marxist theory began its precipitous decline in both the West and in Eastern Europe.) Differentiating himself from Marxism, but by shifting gears – or, to change metaphors, by shifting the focal length rather than by opposing its political aims (or at least the political aims of the anti-Stalinist left) – Foucault chose to research not social structures such as class divisions or the two genders established by patriarchy, but rather the history of the formation of modern knowledges of humanity. His somewhat fragmented account of the emergence of modern knowledges of the human soul and human populations began with research on early psychiatry's transformation of premodern knowledges of madness, the subject of his first two books. The project then expanded to encompass various knowledges of individuals and cultures that developed in the late eighteenth and early nineteenth centuries – from natural history to political economy and public health science, as well as Enlightenment-inspired projects seeking to minimize overt cruelty and reform how criminals are punished.

In his early books on madness and psychiatry, Foucault had argued that psychiatry is actually a product, an effect, of the institutionalization and medicalization of people who came to be seen as mentally ill – instead of the asylum being a project devised by psychiatry to implement its theories. Similarly, Foucault suggested that the applied social sciences emerged as they were needed to serve as rationalizations of various existing practices for governing the marginal, the poor, and the criminal – practices for responding to immediate problems that developed in a contingent manner, unsystematically. Thus, institutionalized enterprises such as social work, urban planning, and penology were not so much debunked by Foucault as de-centred. Foucault did not ask: does social work or public health serve the interests of the ruling class, or could such knowledges help to bring about social change and more equality? That old Marxist question about the 'ideological function' of expert knowledges was set aside. Instead, adapting the term 'problematization', commonly used by French thinkers of the time, Foucault asked instead: how was it that a certain issue (madness, crime, punishment) became seen as a problem requiring attention and management? And what techniques (including techniques of counting, writing, and reporting) were assumed to be useful in the description and the management of the problem in question?

In respect to criminal justice, although Nietzsche is not quoted in *Discipline and Punish*, the book generally follows Nietzsche's view that practices of punishment evolve for a variety of inglorious reasons, and that criminal law, far from being a rational product of the human mind, is an after-the-fact rationalization invented to justify particular forms of cruelty and violence (Nietzsche 1969). Portraying penology, criminal law, and criminology in general as rationalizations of various rather haphazardly chosen practices of confinement, humiliation, and suffering that nineteenth-century Europeans believed to be civilized and enlightened (by contrast to the public infliction of physical punishment used in the past), Foucault's work could be said to pull the rug out from under the feet of criminology as such. Or, to put it differently, for Foucault the term 'critical criminology' is an oxymoron.

Again, Foucault was not interested in uncovering the hidden interests served by this or that mainstream discourse or institution. He was interested in a more empirical question: understanding the way in which particular situations and activities came to be seen as problems calling for solutions; and then analysing the particular constellation of ways of seeing and addressing the problem in question that came to be used to measure, describe, contain, and manage 'the problem' in its diverse manifestations.

To underline the unexpected character of Foucault's success within legal studies and criminology, it has to be first pointed out that *Discipline and Punish* says very little, indeed almost nothing, about the twentieth century. The only modern knowledge that Foucault pursued into the twentieth century in any serious way was economics (Foucault 2008). By contrast, Foucault's account of the history of criminal justice never extends into the present, and is in any case extremely fragmented, with some of his research into classical Greek, medieval, and early modern practices of accusation and witnessing being wholly left out of *Discipline and Punish* and delivered only in lectures that were only published long after his death (as will be discussed in Chapters 6 and 7). But even now that we have a fairly full picture of Foucault's research on prisons, criminal law, criminal justice, and other practices of security and crime control, none of this quite vast, mostly posthumously published work takes us into the twentieth century. Thus, generations of criminology students have been misleadingly told that *Discipline and Punish* is a theoretically oriented 'history of the *modern* penal system' (a typical description, taken from the popular American cheat-notes website Sparknotes; emphasis added), when in fact the book only takes the reader to the point at which criminology was invented, in the 1880s and 1890s.

The reader might well be asking: if the critical analysis of the well-meaning reforms of criminal codes and prisons that took place around the time of the French Revolution and the 'Rights of Man', the analysis presented in *Discipline and Punish*, was not meant as a contribution to criminology or a call for a different kind of criminology, and if his much-vaunted history of the modern penal system abruptly ends somewhere in the middle of the nineteenth century, why did he take so much time and care with it and why is it so influential?

The answer is that the nineteenth-century lunatic asylum and the penitentiary were for Foucault not marginal institutions where marginal people were put away out of sight, but the very opposite. Foucault explains that these institutions were invented by reformers unhappy with the physical punishments and restraints used in the past. These people, including both scientifically oriented doctors and religiously driven reformers, denounced as anti-scientific as well as inhumane the traditional practice of locking away, in the same dungeons or jails, the mad, the convicted, those awaiting trial, and the homeless indigent. The new, airy, relatively spacious specialized institutions that were built at great state expense and came to dot the Victorian landscape (orphanages, asylums for the insane, homes for 'fallen women', etc.) were for Foucault hugely important precisely because, far from being exceptional and marginal, they served as laboratories of mainstream modern governance.

In indoor spaces like penitentiaries – in which 'criminals' were for the first time separated from lunatics, vagrants, abandoned children, and the elderly indigent – the availability of a captive population that was thought to be 'naturally' separate from the types of people held in other types of institutions, and the consequent emergence of intellectual devices to further differentiate the population of prisons and asylums into subcategories, allowed the new experts of the modern soul or 'self' (Rose 1990) to reach into the deepest recesses of human bodies and souls. These 'orthopaedists of individuality', as they are vividly described in *Discipline and Punish*, were able to experiment with and refine methods that, once perfected in the artificial, special-purpose environment of a mental hospital or a reformatory, could be used, in a milder way and with less constant control, on 'normal' populations.

How is this a challenge to criminology's premises? Conservative criminology believes that habitual offenders are indeed abnormal and need special control measures. Left-wing criminologists, on their part, believe that offenders are 'stigmatized', and emphasize the discrimination and prejudice that those suspected of criminality face. But both sides tend to assume that 'crime' can and should be studied separately from other phenomena, and that 'criminals' can in turn be studied as a distinct population. Whether condemning offenders or commiserating with them, therefore, criminologists necessarily carve out their special domain by separating crime and criminals from other issues and other populations.

In sharp contrast to criminology's mandate, Foucault chose to underline those features of the penitentiary that are also found outside its walls. The most celebrated example is no doubt the techniques of 'panoptic' prisoner surveillance that Jeremy Bentham recommended should be implemented in order to facilitate cutbacks in prison staff while maximizing surveillance, techniques which are today used everywhere on both public and private property. But as the next chapter will explain, the nineteenth-century penitentiary also pioneered a number of other key techniques of governance that sought to create self-disciplined subjects out of criminals. By emphasizing the dispersal of techniques invented in prisons to the broader society, Foucault put in question the criminological taken-for-granted practice of treating crime and crime control as separate subjects of inquiry.

It is thus not surprising that when I teach Foucault's concept of 'discipline', the examples that work best to help students understand the concept and appreciate the pervasiveness of the phenomenon tend to be drawn not so much from the criminal justice world but rather from their school, and especially their kindergarten experiences. Being taught the correct way to hold a pencil and the proper way to sit on a chair, so that over time most of the children in the room 'naturally' assume certain standardized, respectable bodily positions, is a common, indeed almost universal experience that, as Foucault argues, disciplines the soul by acting on the body and standardizing its appearance and its conduct. Few people will ever see the inside of a prison, but virtually everyone goes through the subtly disciplinary experience of kindergarten. Foucault's analysis of prisons, therefore, displaces and de-centres the prison, even as it describes many of its characteristics in minute detail.

But did Foucault inadvertently save critical criminology?

It has just been shown that Foucault studied the history of penitentiaries in an anti-criminological manner (just as he had previously studied the history of madness in an anti-psychiatric manner). For some of the mainstream criminal law and criminology scholars who read Foucault or heard about him second hand from the 1970s onward, that meant that Foucault could be safely ignored. At the same time, Foucault's insistence on what prisons and asylums have in common with the rest of the modern world helped boost his image in less traditional circles. Focusing his empirical research on institutions of confinement while blurring the boundaries between the governance of the 'deviant' and the governance of the well-behaved population served to secure his reputation as a creative theorist whose work allowed criminologists to broaden their horizons and include non-penal and even non-state institutions within their purview.

Foucault's insistence on de-centring prisons and crime thus helped those scholars who in the 1980s and after were growing disenchanted with criminology's traditional exclusive focus on criminal law, and were moving to map 'regulation' more broadly. That the subtle, private-sector methods of crowd control and behaviour modification used by the Disney corporation to organize spaces and bodies in Disney World could be read with the same eye that critically studied the actions of the public police – as was done in a very influential piece by criminologists Clifford Shearing and Philip Stenning (1985) – is just one example of the way in which Foucault's de-centring of crime and criminology paradoxically helped revive criminology and give it new life. This was done by making its research relevant to social science generally. Biographical details are always to be taken with a grain of salt, but it may perhaps be worth telling that the Disney World article in question persuaded me – who was then (mid-1980s) a philosophically trained women's studies instructor with no interest whatsoever in criminology – that criminological research might be worth reading.

It would be an exaggeration to claim that, once the 1970s enthusiasm for Marxist and quasi-Marxist analyses faded, critical criminology might have withered away if it had not been for Foucault's eruption. Some other paradigm could well have emerged to reform and retrofit progressive and theoretically oriented criminology: by the 1980s there were a significant number of criminology departments and centres that needed to justify their existence as scholarly enterprises distinct from government policy shops; and necessity would have ensured that some new post-Marxist paradigm was invented or borrowed from one place or another. But it may not be much of an exaggeration to say that without Foucault's work, subsequent critical criminology might well have been theoretically shallow and tired, and would have lost prestige. Would progressive criminologists have managed to find a way out of the ritual repetition of 'class, race, and gender' and the interminable arguments about whether disability, aboriginality, and other factors can be incorporated into the existing class–race–gender paradigm, and, if so how – arguments that leave intact the structuralist epistemology that underpinned the critical criminology of the 1960s and 1970s? Perhaps. But, as it happened, Foucault's work was for many the life raft that took progressive criminology away from the sinking ship of neo-Marxism. We will return to the question of where criminology was when *Discipline and Punish* became a hit in Chapter 2; and there I will explain what I mean by 'structuralist epistemology' (and by 'neo-Marxism'), so I can here reassure readers who are not familiar with those terms that they need not become anxious. But before we move into that discussion, it is necessary to make some additional general methodological comments that will help readers not only to learn something about Foucault but also to have the information that is necessary in order to read Foucault's works properly (since his published works are notable for not explaining themselves and their method, as is the norm for works of 'theory').

Choosing an object of study: persons, institutions, or practices

During the first century of its existence (1880s to 1980s), criminology's main aim was to isolate and scientifically study certain groups of offenders (mainly repeat/habitual offenders and/or those who commit violent crimes without an obvious economic motive). In general, while criminal law focuses strictly on particular *acts*, banning some and leaving the rest ungoverned, criminology has tended to be more interested in the *person* who commits illegal and especially violent illegal acts; or, more precisely, the *type of person* who can be said to be likely to commit such acts – whether such persons/types are identified through inherited traits or certain sociological characteristics (family upbringing, neighbourhood, peer group, etc.)

Persons and their propensities can in turn be seen and governed either as individuals or as groups. Some criminologists, of a psychological bent, focus on actual persons in order to diagnose and perhaps suggest treatments for their criminal tendencies. Other more sociologically oriented criminologists study the 'risk factors' that, on average, cause crime and/or other socially undesirable activities to increase or decrease. Sociological criminologists these days often study neighbourhood-based groups or youth peer groups, usually comparing one group to another in order to draw general conclusions about social cohesion, crime rates, recidivism rates, resilience, and risk factors.

While this traditional focus on persons and types of person lives on in today's criminology, there has been another strand that became particularly popular from the 1960s onward: the study of the institutions of criminal justice. Much of this work was spurred by the symbolic interactionism of the 1960s, which, turning criminology's gaze around, explained that people and groups can come to look and even behave differently or in a deviant way as a result of being stigmatized by the very authorities who then claim to be surprised at discovering that crime or deviance exists among those groups. That 'the criminal' is a figure that is defined and even created by the actions of police and other criminal justice institutions – rather than being a naturally occurring entity – was an insight of great fruitfulness, leading to hundreds of studies with such titles as 'the social construction of delinquency', 'the social construction of crime', 'the social construction of women's sexuality', etc.

As part of this trend towards understanding social problems as 'socially constructed', many progressive criminologists chose to focus their critical gaze not on criminals and their communities but rather on the powerful institutions that are supposedly needed by every 'civilized' society to govern crime. Many argued that these institutions actually produce crime through marginalization, stigma, economic deprivation, prejudice, etc. University courses in criminology were not very numerous then (the 1970s); but in those few institutions that had separate criminology programmes or departments, courses on 'policing' and 'the courts' were created. And 'penology' – previously a managerial pursuit dominated by prison officials, doctors, lawyers, and judges – became academically respectable by being turned into the critical study of imprisonment and other practices of state punishment.

Foucault's work, or rather his book *Discipline and Punish*, quickly became a great resource for those progressive and theoretically minded instructors who wanted to give 'penology' a new, critical twist. But incorporating some of Foucault's insights into the existing organization of criminological knowledge may have deprived generations of students of the opportunity to critically reflect on assumptions about what should be studied, assumptions that are invisible because they are presupposed by the programmes in which they study. A key such fundamental assumption is that scholars interested in law, crime, and justice will naturally study *acts* and their consequences (as criminal law does); *persons* (either individually or as part of groups); and/or *institutions* (as explained immediately above). Those three choices may seem quite sufficient, encompassing almost everything one might want to study. However, a major reason why Foucault revolutionized not only the study of crime and security but also a whole range of fields – from social work and the sociology of medicine to philosophy – is that he refused to answer or even to contemplate the usual 'acts, persons, or institutions' multiple choice question.

Some of Foucault's early work sought to trace the emergence of modern systems of knowledge across a wide range of areas, and terms such as 'discourse' and 'episteme' were efforts to describe the object of these studies. Without going into details, that early work was interested in uncovering how certain rules for what can be said came to be, especially what can be said authoritatively by highbrow institutions. Why and how certain issues came to the fore at certain times, and what questions were thought to be the 'natural' ones to ask and ponder: this is the sort of thing that preoccupied Foucault in his early phase, concerned with what he later called 'the history of systems of thought'. 'Systems' here meant not so much the explicit content of formal knowledges but rather the underlying shifts that turned something previously taken for granted into a problem, and prompted people to analyse it following certain assumptions about how knowledge is to be obtained.

But as his work turned somewhat away from the philosophical and literary interests of his student days and acquired a more concrete historical character (from the early 1970s onward), he became increasingly interested in the everyday practices that, in his view, defined an era or a social system as much or more than ideologies and explicit systems of thought. Making particular *practices* or *techniques for governing people and problems* into the main object of research and analysis, and hence refusing the 'acts, persons, or institutions' classification that had seemed sufficient to others, is arguably Foucault's key methodological innovation, in relation to criminology and legal studies at any rate.

What is particularly striking is that Foucault's decision to focus on practices – especially on the practices that came to be called 'techniques of governance', which included physical arrangements like the panopticon but also ways of arranging information, such as case files – did not come from an engagement with social science research. Somewhat oddly, he never seems to have had much time for either anthropology or sociology. His interest in studying practices seems to have developed in large part (at the biographical level) out of being increasingly drawn to archival research. He came to enjoy poring over government reports, pamphlets written by obscure people who designed and ran asylums and other institutions, public health inquiries, and all manner of other documents instead of sitting at home reading books written by the philosophers and established intellectuals, as one would have expected from his traditionally French and hence highly philosophical education. But the important methodological decision to make 'practices' the object of study and analysis also came, somewhat paradoxically, from a philosophical inspiration: Nietzsche.

Nietzsche had famously argued that the history of philosophy, and European thought more generally, is not an orderly progression of rational arguments being replaced by other arguments, as one might think from philosophy textbooks. The history of European thought is rather a kind of Greek tragedy in which people and whole cultures act first and think later, and in which a particular practice motivated by nothing more than cruelty or simple practical convenience – the practice of physically punishing those who have not paid their debts, for example – is justified after the fact with elaborate theories. And in a collection of fragments that in my view is the most 'Foucaultian' of all his works, *Human, All Too Human*, Nietzsche takes this further by arguing, totally against the grain of criminal law theory, that the very theory of 'free will' as an essential feature of humans was invented to retroactively justify punishing criminals. Why? Because to make punishment seem fair and just one had to claim that they had wilfully made 'wrong' choices (Nietzsche 1996, Part II, Sections 22–4: 311–13).

Foucault was highly influenced by Nietzsche's claim that highbrow knowledges may be best described as *ex post facto* rationalizations of self-interested or even cruel practices, and that practices and habitual ways of doing things and addressing problems that are adopted without much deliberation by numerous institutions and even by individuals may well evolve for quite contingent reasons, as those at the front lines of managing people and problems try out new ways of doing things or borrow ideas from other contexts. Nietzsche's cynical view of the history of philosophy and theology was thus used to undercut the functionalist reasoning common in the social sciences at that time (and into today). Functionalism is the fallacy that assumes that if a particular institution or practice serves a certain purpose (e.g. parenting helps political authorities because parents work for free to produce good, disciplined citizens), then the purpose that something serves is its cause, its *raison d'être* (e.g. the family is theorized as an institution of social control). Nietzsche stressed that the function played by an institution or practice today in no way explains its origin, and that, in turn, the historical origin of an idea or institution does not determine what future purpose it might serve.

Foucault takes Nietzsche's anti-functionalism into the realm of social science research, and undertakes to show that all manner of social practices that may well grease certain political or social wheels have had chequered careers, and have been reinvented to serve a variety of objectives. Techniques of governance are flexible; they can be separated from the larger institutional context in which they were born and recycled in quite different contexts for different goals. A Marxist analysis, for instance, would tend to claim that clocks were invented to discipline workers into punctuality. Foucault does not deny that clocks do as a matter of fact serve that purpose; but he insists that there is nothing inevitable about that particular function or effect. Measuring time objectively and quantitatively by means of clocks was in fact initially a solution to the problem of how to get a large group of monks, in early modern Europe, to all show up for prayer in the chapel six times a day. Individual prayer does not need any time machine; but monasteries were based on the theory that a group that prayed and worked and ate all together at the same time served a unique spiritual purpose.

Once manufacturing developed, clocks became useful for different reasons, and were placed atop factories to govern workers (and their families) quite coercively, with wages being deducted for lateness. Making clocks and using them to measure time and govern people through quantified time is thus one practice that was invented in one place to solve a highly specific problem (assembling monks efficiently), but that was later found to be highly useful for other quite different purposes. The history of time-telling bells and clocks that Foucault would have written if he had devoted sufficient energy to the task (instead of simply scattering some telling comments in various texts) would emphasize the ways in which the same technology can migrate from one type of institution to another, and be recycled for new uses.

Practices are not infinitely flexible and adaptable, however. The measurement of time by means of clocks – clocks that initially were sovereigns of their own monastery or village but eventually had to be synchronized with one another to facilitate modern transportation – is a practice that has certain affinities for particular ways of seeing the world, particular ways of arranging people and arranging things and spaces. Clocks standardize the day (and the night), rendering all minutes and hours homogenous and equal. They remove time-keeping from its ancient basis in natural cycles and seasons; and, not coincidentally, they facilitate and indeed encourage the standardization of human conduct. The monastery clock calling monks to prayer; the factory or town hall clock telling workers to hurry to their jobs; the school opening bell: these otherwise different instances of time-keeping share a certain governing logic. By means of this invention, people as well as time itself are homogenized and 'synchronized' through a subtle technique that seems quite impersonal. The authorities that organize time in homogenous, abstract, equal quantities and impose penalties for lateness hide behind the clock, as it were. While of course a monastery clock has a certain spiritual basis and objective, whereas the factory clock serves the profit motive, the clock itself is not wholly neutral – it is an invention that can be seen as harbouring 'disciplinary' tendencies or possibilities.

But Foucault would never have drawn a general affirmative conclusion along the lines of 'clocks *are* disciplinary'. Any particular practice (clocks, uniforms, roll calls, schedules) can always be repurposed in a different governing system, and used to accomplish different purposes. A good example would be a CCTV camera placed outside a women's shelter, facing out to the street. Whereas most critical criminologists think of video surveillance as always and necessarily serving the interests of the powers that be, that particular CCTV camera actually empowers the battered women living in the shelter. If the CCTV footage is turned over to the police so they can lay charges against a violent husband who was prowling outside the shelter, then the footage would acquire certain disciplinary functions; but if it is used only to help assaulted women feel and be safer, the camera and its images could hardly be said to constitute an example of discipline and surveillance.

In general, Foucault is always interested in seeing how a technique invented in one type of institution is borrowed elsewhere – a methodological approach that would later give rise to a large literature on the spread, across institutions, of modern techniques of governance, from the audit to the risk assessment scale.

Not power/knowledge but powers/knowledges

Having discussed at some length the importance of Foucault's methodological decision to make governing practices his object of study from the early 1970s onward, it is now time to address the other key methodological issue: the equally Nietzschean question of the close relationship between power and knowledge. As is well known, Nietzsche debunked Western philosophy by arguing that all knowledge projects, including the pursuit of 'pure' philosophical knowledge, is always already an exercise of power, regardless of if or how that knowledge is then put to use in the practical world. In keeping with Nietzsche's view of knowledges generally as forms of power – and also supported by research being then carried out by others on such topics as the history of statistics– Foucault argued that any systematic, rational knowledge project wields a certain power in itself, even before being put to use. Counting the inhabitants of a kingdom for purposes of a census, for example, is an exercise of state power, whether or not the census data are then used to impose taxes or for other purposes. Measuring the height of every male called up for military service, to give another example, may or may not have any consequences for the recruits themselves; but the data collected constitute a knowledge of the male population at a particular point in time that is also a particular kind of power. Knowing the average height and weight, and knowing which parts of the country or which subpopulations are stronger and healthier than others, is power – as today's practitioners of 'data mining' well know.

Foucault often used the term 'power/knowledge' to indicate a more or less systematic collection of discourses and practices that share a particular logic, with the overall premise being that any form of power that has some intellectual justification (as distinct from brute force, which for Foucault is not a form of 'power' in his sense) is inextricable from a particular type of knowledge.

In medicine, for example, Foucault distinguished between clinical knowledge – which is focused on 'reading' a person's symptoms and, using prior case histories, producing a diagnosis – and epidemiology: population-based knowledges of health that aggregate data in order to produce morbidity and mortality *rates*. The clinical gaze and the epidemiological gaze are quite distinct, for Foucault, even though they are both medical knowledge projects. The power of the wise clinician over the individual patient is in turn differentiated from the power over the population exercised by the data-collecting scientist. Similarly, a forensic psychiatrist's knowledge of the likely behaviour of a particular offender is, for Foucault, qualitatively different from a sociological criminologist's knowledge of crime rates. Different ways of gathering and authorizing knowledge constitute different types of power.

The key point here is that Foucault distinguishes himself from Nietzsche and the Nietzschean tradition by emphasizing the plurality and heterogeneity of knowledges and powers. Nietzsche famously generalized about a nearly universal 'will to power'; Foucault, especially in his later years, eschewed such generalizations in favour of documenting the plurality of powers/knowledges. In regard to the data mining example mentioned above, for instance, if Foucault had lived long enough to see the phenomenon, he would have been interested in the differences between personalized, highly visible ways of collecting information about individuals (the form filled out by the door-to-door census taker, say) and the impersonal, even automated, collection of information that is gathered from one's credit card or one's computer and aggregated so as to form part of a set of numbers that has some commercial or government use. Both exercises involve gathering personal information about individuals; but Foucault would be more interested in the differences between them than in the similarities.

How many modes of power/knowledge are there?

Some accounts of Foucault's work claim that Foucault divides power/knowledge into three forms or modes: sovereignty, discipline, and governmentality. This claim is not quite accurate, as I will show shortly; but first it is worth explaining what these three terms mean, since they are indeed crucial in Foucault's work. 'Sovereignty' is a term used by Foucault to describe a top-down form of power that is static, in the sense that preserving the authority and majesty of the ruler is what matters, not reforming anything or anyone. Sovereignty does not require much if any knowledge of the characteristics of the subjects; and, importantly, sovereignty proceeds by prohibiting certain acts and taking power away from those who break the rules or otherwise threaten the powers that be. Sovereign power is typically exercised by centralized states; but there can be private sovereigns – church leaders, for example, or, depending on the situation, the heads of households or families. Today, the Catholic Church is one organization that can be taken to exemplify sovereignty: bishops have some autonomous power, but they are all appointed by the Pope. The rules of the church do not have a police force behind them; but the Pope, like Hobbes' Leviathan, has the power to decide whom to excommunicate. The Catholic Church of course is complex and heterogeneous from the governance point of view, as all major organizations are, and has various internal mechanisms and projects that go well beyond sovereignty; it would not have survived if it had been an exclusively sovereign enterprise. But the Pope's authority to dictate moral law, implicitly acknowledged in the reverence and awe that is visible in papal trips around the world, can be seen as an example of sovereignty.

By contrast, 'discipline' refers to a type of power that is not merely concerned to preserve its own top-down authority, but rather seeks to reform people as well as control and improve or maximize spaces and territories. Discipline thus requires some knowledge of individuals, who are measured and 'normalized' by means of bell curving and other mechanisms, operations that all differentiate people from one another rather than treating everyone in a territory as abstractly equal subjects of an earthly or spiritual kingdom, as sovereigns do. Religious as well as secular methods to probe the human soul and improve the human body, from Catholic confession to fitness classes, are generally 'disciplinary' (though other logics might be at work as well). Psychology, social work, psychotherapy, and their amateur equivalents from the television talk show to the Alcoholics Anonymous group, are the typical knowledges of a 'disciplinary' society.

In turn, 'governmentality' (a term invented late in Foucault's career, and that never saw the light of published day during his life) can, in a rough way, be said to refer to ways of governing that are less intrusive and personal than discipline, and that rely more on managing risks, organizing spaces to minimize disorder and opportunities for crime, maximizing resources, and planning for the future. Somewhat confusingly for readers, governmentality as used by Foucault is not tied up with government in the sense of state institutions. Foucault relies on older meanings of the word 'to govern', as in the 'governor' found on boats or the Victorian phrase 'a well-governed mind'. One feature that will be explored later in the book is that while sovereignty is mainly concerned with preserving authority, governmentality is future oriented and embraces change (as long as the change goes in the direction of maximizing resources and minimizing losses).

Risk assessments of all kinds, from the environmental assessments required for infrastructure projects to the 'risk scales' used in parole and probation, are typical ways of gathering and using knowledge that promote or enact what Foucault calls governmentality. To give another example: crime prevention through environmental design is a perfect example of 'governmental' thinking. Its clear contrast with sending someone to prison to be reformed perfectly illustrates the shift in logic from discipline to governmentality. Instead of working intensively to create good citizens and workers one individual at a time, as disciplinary organizations do, governmentality refers to a 'mentality of government' that manages risks in a more impersonal, future-oriented, and aggregate manner. Statistics, probability calculations, performance assessments, and audits of organizations are typical governmental knowledge forms.

Contrary to popular opinion, Foucault did not believe that these three modes or forms of power (and the knowledges associated with them) constitute a complete list; but before we take up the question of other forms of power/knowledge beyond those three, let us pause for a moment to consider the two examples illustrating the differences between these three modes that Foucault himself gave in the introductory lecture of his 1977–78 series of Collège de France lectures (Foucault 2007).

The first example given in the January 11, 1978 lecture, conveniently for this book, is a criminal-law example. Foucault explains that how theft is seen and governed depends on the prevailing mode of power/knowledge. If theft is governed by a 'simple prohibition' such as 'you must not kill, you must not steal' (ibid.: 4) – with the punishment being fixed in advance rather than tailor-made for particular individuals – then we have a sovereign or 'juridical' mechanism. (Note that in French *juridique* has the same meaning as the English term 'legal' does in the phrase 'legal studies', that is, pertaining to law in general rather than to a particular law; arguably, the English text should read 'legal' rather than the more scholarly sounding 'juridical'.) Be that as it may, it is clear that here the power flows top-down exclusively and is exercised only sporadically, when the sovereign is threatened (and crime is in turn defined as an attack on the sovereign's order, as in 'breach of the King's peace'). When that power is exercised by the sovereign, it is against the subject, the citizen: sovereign power prohibits and punishes, and thus limits the autonomy and movement of the ordinary person.

If one governs theft and the possibility of future thefts in a 'disciplinary' manner, by contrast, there are 'supervisions, checks, inspections' (ibid.: 4) that seek to identify the deviant minority that is likely to steal. Similar mechanisms are in place during the punishment phase, when offenders, instead of merely being punished (say, by flogging) are 'reformed' and 'rehabilitated'. Prison labour, prison prayers, and, later, psychological testing are all disciplinary techniques that differentiate criminals from ordinary people and that differentiate different types of criminal from one another. Disciplinary measures thus differentiate, whereas in the face of the sovereign, all subjects are treated equally and without any individualized knowledge. In regard to knowledge forms, the case file that follows the criminal around is a creature of – and essential knowledge format for – discipline. Not coincidentally, doctors have case files on patients too, as do schools for students. Medieval sovereigns, on their part, had no need of case files. 'Surveillance, diagnosis, and the possible transformation of individuals' (ibid.: 5) are the aims and indeed the substance of disciplinary mechanisms.

And what about governmentality? The term stresses the differences between the kinds of power and knowledge practised in penitentiaries and old-fashioned schools, on the one hand, and on the other hand the impersonal management of risks in the aggregate that became increasingly important in the twentieth century, as direct discipline became both questionable from a human rights perspective and simply too expensive from a fiscal perspective. Governing theft from the standpoint of governmentality, Foucault tells his listeners, involves measuring not so much individual thefts as rates of theft.

> Are there times, regions, and penal systems that will increase or reduce this average rate? …how much does this criminality cost society, what damage does it cause, or loss of earnings, and so on? Further questions: what is the cost of repressing these thefts?'
>
> (Foucault 2007: 5)

While sovereignty's typical format is the criminal code (or religious equivalents such as the Ten Commandments), and disciplinary mechanisms love schedules and norms that mould individual conduct, what Foucault here wavers between calling 'governmentality' and 'an apparatus of security' (Foucault 2007: 6) seeks to govern risks and lower rates of offending by whatever means are empirically demonstrated to work, regardless of whether they have the effect of reforming or deterring individuals or whether they simply work around individuals (as in the example of crime prevention through environmental design).

Foucault later gives a different example, from the realm of urban design. Sovereignty was embodied in the royal or imperial city, with its static hierarchical plan designed to reinforce the majesty of a single central point of power (the Forbidden City in Beijing is the best example I know of this, though Foucault does not mention it). Beyond the walls of the royal palace, other inhabitants and households are arranged as in a royal banquet, in descending order of importance, until one reaches the lowly peasantry in the countryside. In early modern Europe, however, ambitious visionaries designed utopian cities from scratch, borrowing some ideas from Roman encampments but expanding the orderly spatial logic of the Roman military camp to include civil society. In the disciplinary city, urban space came to be treated as important in itself, not merely as the area that happens to be around the royal palace. The key problem that now emerges as requiring solution in the 'disciplinary city' is circulation. Medieval cities had notoriously narrow, winding, hard-to-know streets. The urban designers (and the garden designers) of the eighteenth century disliked that aesthetic, and instead sought to create wide, straight avenues and symmetrical squares. In this way the town would be 'a perfect agent of circulation' as well as a visible manifestation of symmetry and discipline. 'Sovereignty capitalizes a territory … whereas discipline structures a space' (Foucault 2007: 17, 20).

How governmentality is embodied in urban design is not as clear in Foucault's lecture, but one gathers that the governmental city may not look as elegant as a classic eighteenth-century town such as Jane Austen's Bath. Aesthetics gives way to a concern with functionality and efficiency. A governmental city has proper sewers and an efficient transportation system, and a governmental city uses evidence to plan its future and its infrastructure. The current practice of comparing cities to one another by ranking them according to certain 'indicators', which did not exist when Foucault was giving this lecture, is a perfect example of the governmental city. Neither royal splendour nor symmetrical park design is valued in the governmental city; what is now valued are efficiency, rapidity and ease of movement (especially for economic purposes), and socioeconomic data that (ideally) forecasts a prosperous future.

The tripartite sovereignty–discipline–governmentality division (which has an unfortunate formal resemblance to Marx's theory about feudalism, capitalism, and socialism, as well as to Hegel's division of the family, civil society, and the state) is indeed made by Foucault on a few occasions apart from the lecture just cited. But all of these, it needs to be pointed out, were lectures, not polished publications. If one puts together the 'sovereignty, discipline, governmentality' categorization found in several of the posthumously published public lectures with other statements about other forms of power/knowledge that are found in diverse writings and interviews, one can see that, unlike other theorists of 'modernity', Foucault never claimed to have produced a final and exhaustive classification.

Just to give two examples that complicate the picture, we can mention two modes of power/knowledge that do not fall squarely either inside or outside the three just mentioned. One is 'biopolitics', which is related to discipline but which is discussed quite separately, especially in *The History of Sexuality Volume I* (1980). As will be explained at more length in Chapter 3, biopolitical power is exercised over populations, but without necessarily aiming to reform individuals or control deviants. If and when individuals are acted upon biopolitically (as in family planning programmes in parts of the global South), the individual is not governed to improve or reform him/her, but becomes merely a means to a population-level end. Encouraging someone to have babies or to not have them could be disciplinary if the aim is to govern the individual and their family, as when the Catholic Church preaches against contraception (the Catholic Church is not particularly interested in the biopolitical consequences of its views on birth control); but such advice becomes biopolitical if the main aim is to increase or lower the population.

Furthermore, biopolitics can work to increase health, as in universal vaccination programmes or as in using drinking water to silently convey fluoride to human bodies. But it can also be detrimental to individuals, as in the compulsory sterilization of intellectually disabled individuals, or, in the extreme, in genocidal programmes to 'ethnically cleanse' or physically eliminate one subpopulation for the sake of the health of the larger nation or state. In the twentieth century, Foucault famously said, wars came to be fought not in the name of the sovereign but in the name of the population, and even massacres of a domestic subpopulation are justified as quasi public health measures.

Biopolitics can and does coexist with either discipline or governmentality, and can thus be regarded as analytically autonomous (though some scholars try hard to make it fit into one of the three more familiar types of power/knowledge). And it is not the only form of power/knowledge that drew Foucault's interest and that cannot easily be stuffed into the tripartite division. One that has particular relevance to criminology is *pastoral power*.

While Greek societies were developing political forms and political theories, based on the urban institution of 'the polis', Foucault (2007) points out that there were peoples that did not privilege building cities and securing territory, and instead saw the members of a national or political group as a 'flock' unified by a shepherd-like leader (see lectures of February 8, 15, and 22, and March 1, 1978). Abraham and his descendants are the paradigm here, as the Greeks are the paradigm case for the contrasting political game of cities and citizens. The Jewish people were united not so much through claiming a territory or building great cities as through being led by one charismatic leader after another. The pastoral legacy of the people as a flock in need of a shepherd was continued by Christianity, Foucault argues, with church leaders admitting that political power may well rest with kings who control territories, but that church authority (seen as qualitatively different from political rule) is vested in leaders whose power lies in their ability and willingness to go and rescue 'lost sheep'.

The pastoral leader does not count up wealth or quantitatively measure improvements and deviations; the power of the shepherd is individual, embodied, and highly personalized, and stands in very sharp contrast to the numerical calculations and risk assessments of contemporary governmentality.

Some criminologists have pointed out that despite Foucault's insistence on prisons as laboratories of discipline, in many instances penitentiary inmates are in fact governed by spiritually motivated 'shepherds' (from chaplains to lay volunteers) as much or more than by file-wielding doctors and *Diagnostic and Statistical Manual* (DSM)-centred psychologists. In women's prisons especially, Foucault's notion of pastoral power is one potentially useful way of describing the authority of successful prison matrons, lady prison visitors, 12-step group leaders, and volunteers motivated by feminist ideas about sisterhood and support. In general, pastoral power is anti-quantification and anti-efficiency.

When we think about everyday interactions in prisons and in probation and parole programmes, it is very clear that to see any one realm – here, criminal justice – as adequately mapped by imposing a rigid framework where sovereignty gives way to discipline which in turn is abandoned in favour of governmentality is inadequate. Not only do exercises of top-down prohibitory power without any reformatory aims still exist, but also there are numerous programmes and techniques that cannot be easily characterized as either disciplinary or governmental, or even a combination of both. Pastoral power is alive and well (as twelve-step recovery programmes show); and while biopower may be rather in the background in the criminal justice context, one can nevertheless see that logic at work in various programmes that are designed more to maintain the health of the population as a whole than to look after individual needs.

In general, it is very important to avoid seeing Foucault's experiments with various ways of naming different kinds of power/knowledge as a rigid classification. First of all, no one institution is ever a 'pure' example of any one type of power. An insurance company, for example, is primarily organized to serve governmental ends; but within the organization itself, any number of other modes of power and knowledge may and probably do exist, creating bonds or hostilities between workers and employers and among the different groups. And the customers of the insurance company may be mere numbers or risk factors as long as they are paying their premiums; but once they make a claim, they too might be disciplined in classic Foucaultian ways. The life of any institution or any set of human relations is always too complex and too mobile and unpredictable to be properly understood by being classified as 'an example of discipline'.

Foucault, tellingly, does not provide definitions for his key terms. He provides descriptions, characterizations, and examples; but these are always in process, always somewhat tentative, and they do not remain static and wholly consistent from one lecture or one published work to another. His great aim was to follow in Nietzsche's footsteps and capture in thought – as far as is humanly possible, which is not very far – the dynamism and unpredictability of life. That meant that his terms and ideas had to themselves be flexible and mobile. Textbook definitions are appropriate for thinkers who want to classify the world once and for all, and elaborate a system where concepts are connected to one another in stable patterns. In the case of Foucault, his desire to always question his own work and dig deeper into his own assumptions created a certain textual elusiveness that frustrates readers, but that even a work designed to explain his thought – such as this book – must try to respect.

Bibliography

Foucault, Michel. 1965. *Madness and Civilization: A History of Insanity in the Age of Reason.* Translated by Richard Howard. New York: Pantheon.

Foucault, Michel. 1970. *The Order of Things: An Archaeology of the Human Sciences.* Translated from the French. London: Tavistock.

Foucault, Michel. 1973. *The Birth of the Clinic: An Archaeology of Medical Perception.* Translated by A. M. Sheridan Smith. New York: Pantheon.

Foucault, Michel. 1977. *Discipline and Punish: The Birth of the Prison.* Translated by Alan Sheridan. New York: Vintage.

Foucault, Michel. 1980. *The History of Sexuality, Vol. I: An Introduction.* Translated by Robert Hurley. New York: Vintage.

Foucault, Michel. 1984. *The History of Sexuality, Vol. II: The Use of Pleasure.* Translated by Robert Hurley. New York: Vintage.

Foucault, Michel. 1988. *The History of Sexuality, Vol. III: The Care of the Self.* Translated by Robert Hurley. New York: Vintage.

Foucault, Michel. 2007. *Security, Territory, Population: Lectures at the* Collège *de France, 1977–1978.* Edited by Michel Senellart. Translated by Graham Burchell. New York: Picador/Palgrave Macmillan.

Foucault, Michel. 2008. *The Birth of Biopolitics: Lectures at the Collège de France, 1978–1979.* Edited by Michel Senellart. Translated by Graham Burchell. New York: Picador.

Garland, David. 1990. *Punishment and Modern Society: A Study in Social Theory.* Oxford: Clarendon.

Macey, David. 1993. *The Lives of Michel Foucault.* London: Hutchinson.

Melossi, Dario. 1990. *The State of Social Control: A Sociological Study of Concepts of State and Social Control in the Making of Democracy*. New York: St. Martin's Press.

Nietzsche, Friedrich. 1969. *On the Genealogy of Morals*. Translated by Walter Kaufman and R. J. Hollingdale. New York: Vintage.

Nietzsche, Friedrich. 1996. *Human, All Too Human: A Book of Free Spirits*. Translated by R. J. Hollingdale. Cambridge, New York: Cambridge University Press.

Rose, Nikolas. 1990. *Governing the Soul: The Shaping of the Private Self*. London, New York: Routledge.

Rose, Nikolas, Pat O'Malley, and Mariana Valverde. 2006. 'Governmentality.' *Annual Review of Law and Social Science* 2(1): 83–104.

Shearing, Clifford and Philip Stenning. 1985. 'From the Panopticon to Disney World: the Development of Discipline,' in Anthony N. Doob and Edward L. Greenspan, eds, *Perspectives in Criminal Law: Essays in Honour of John LL.J. Edwards*. Aurora, Ont.: Canada Law Books, pp. 336–349.

Valverde, Mariana. 2010. 'Specters of Foucault in Law and Society Scholarship.' *Annual Review of Law and Social Science* 6(1): 45–59.

Veyne, Paul. 2010. *Foucault: His Thought, His Character*. Translated by Janet Lloyd. Cambridge: Polity.

Chapter 2

Foucault on the social relations of punishing, 'surveilling' and disciplining

This chapter will be devoted to the work that made Foucault famous among those who study criminal law and criminology – the book published in English under the title *Discipline and Punish*, but whose original title was the slightly different: *Surveiller et Punir*. A brief comment on the translation of the title will help introduce my own argument about what the book does and how it has been read, an argument developed throughout this chapter.

First, the French original title is very clearly a combination of two verbs – or, more accurately as it becomes clear as soon as one starts reading the book, a contrast between them. The first verb, *surveiller*, cannot be directly translated into English: the English noun 'surveillance' has not traditionally had a corresponding verb. Possibly because of Foucault's influence, the *Oxford English Dictionary* (OED) now admits the verb 'to surveil' as an offshoot of 'surveillance'; but *Chambers Dictionary* does not. Just as importantly (and less pedantically), the English noun 'surveillance' has different, more negative connotations than its French equivalent. In English 'surveillance' has Orwellian tones, and evokes ordinary people being monitored by authorities or corporations. But the French word is not always redolent of top-down control. For example, at airports and train stations French people are exhorted to *surveiller* their own baggage, and in French-speaking parks parents may be reminded that they need to *surveiller* their children. *Surveiller*, in French, can refer simply to the everyday need for all of us to exercise ordinary prudence and keep an eye on things.

Alan Sheridan, who not only translated the book but also knew Foucault well, states in his 'translator's note' that 'our noun "surveillance" has an altogether too restricted and technical use.' But a better way of explaining the translation problem would have been to say that 'surveillance', in English, is a term that refers to a top-down gaze whose objective is spatial and social control, whereas in French the term can refer to the mundane need to keep an eye on one's belongings or one's family. Sheridan goes on to say that in the face of the translation difficulties, Foucault himself suggested the English title *Discipline and Punish*. This choice has the virtue of highlighting the book's key term – discipline. However, Foucault, who was not very fluent in English until late in life, may not have fully realized that, in English, if one uses the infinitive of a verb but without including 'to', what was meant as a verb can end up sounding like a thing, a noun. While 'punish' is clearly short for the verb 'to punish', 'discipline' sounds to the Anglophone ear like a noun, a clearly demarcated concept that can be defined once and for all. If one wanted to unambiguously name the *activity of disciplining* to emphasize the interactive and indeed constitutive character of the relationships in question, the translation would have had to read 'To discipline and to punish' – although the publisher would probably have objected to such an awkward title.

The choice to translate the verb *surveiller* by the word 'discipline' had the rather predictable effect of reifying (that is, 'thingifying') the book's key term.[1] 'Discipline' was taken up as a noun by subsequent generations of readers. This point is not a trivial scholarly quibble. As mentioned in the previous chapter, and as will be argued throughout this book, I hold that emphasizing the *relationality* of all forms of power is a central philosophical aim in all of Foucault's work. By contrast to the simplistic version of Marxism that holds that the dominant class, in each mode of production, possesses all the power, cultural as well as economic, or the old radical feminist notion that patriarchy is timeless and men have all the power, Foucault sees power relations as interactive, dynamic, always in process, multifarious and somewhat unpredictable. Power is not like money, a finite entity that some people have and others lack. Power exists only in and through relationships, and the game of power is not a zero-sum game; different groups can be adding to their various forms of power at the same time.

Now, 'to punish' is clearly a relational notion. Dungeons and handcuffs – and for that matter teachers' orders to stay after school – do not themselves punish: punishment only exists in embodied relationships that require constant attention and continuous financial, human and technical support from the institutions authorized to punish. With some exceptions (such as where mafias have more power than governments), states can ensure that punishments actually occur. But that says more about states than about punishment. Many a parent has found that it is one thing to declare that a punishment exists and another to carry it out. *Punishment activities* are thus intersubjective and relational.

By contrast, the relational and thus ever-contingent character of *disciplinary activities* has been obscured in many renderings of Foucault's ideas. Discipline is often described as a type of power that, once invented, inevitably hardens into certain forms that then proliferate like mosquitoes or weeds. This naturalistic way of thinking about discipline is highly problematic from a social science point of view, and in any case is totally at odds with Foucault's philosophical sensibilities. Real-life, constantly negotiated, concrete social relations are obscured and reduced to caricature when they are said to be 'examples' of discipline, as if discipline were a Platonic Idea rather than a generalization elaborated from concrete historical events.

But in fairness to a generation of commentators, it must be admitted that the overly static 'thing-ified' misreading of the central notion of Foucault's book is not to be blamed only on the peculiarities of translation and the oversimplifications inherent in the textbook genre. Foucault's unexplained choice to rely to a very large extent on highly vivid images and long quotes from documents rather than on 'normal' theoretical and methodological explanations also had its own, perhaps unintended, consequences.[2] In *Discipline and Punish*, Foucault made the deliberate and no doubt carefully thought-out choice to memorably describe numerous innovations that had clear disciplinary effects – while largely neglecting to document the failures that dogged every prison administrator and correctional innovator. Foucault also made a point to exclude from this particular book discussions of the unpredictable later careers of recycled disciplinary inventions, disciplinary relationships, and disciplinary techniques. Choosing elegance and simplicity over historical accuracy and the documentation of subsequent unintended consequences (to the dismay of French social historians),[3] Foucault's choice of illustrative vignettes contributed to creating the oversimplified impression that 'discipline' is a noun indicating a fully formed type of society, or even an historical age.

In his lectures at the *Collège de France* (which did not start to appear in print until the late 1990s), Foucault often emphasized the contingency of relations of power/knowledge, and occasionally reminded his audience that different types of power/knowledge can and do coexist. But the books published during his lifetime tended to be narrowly focused and argued, with a single internally coherent original argument being pursued at the expense of acknowledging conflicts amongst authorities, governance failures, and the multiple ways in which both political realities and popular beliefs undercut expert-created governance innovations (Geertz 1978). And, of all of the books published during his lifetime, *Discipline and Punish* had the simplest argument.

Striking a middle ground between mere summary/commentary and a retrospective critique, this chapter attempts simultaneously to explain the key insights of *Discipline and Punish* and to give readers some sense of how subsequent scholarship has made it possible to see the limits of Foucault's book, while still acknowledging its brilliance. But before proceeding to the commentary on the book, a note on its political and activist context is necessary.

Political context: Foucault's anti-prison activism

From late 1970 to mid-1973, Foucault did far less research and academic writing than at any other time in his life. The reason was that, along with other intellectuals of the 1968 generation, he chose to put much effort into activist endeavours. Previously, he had had some involvement with the radical student protests of the late 1960s. But after he was appointed professor at the brand-new, left-wing university of Vincennes in the autumn of 1968 – and experienced at first hand the constant disruptions to learning caused by student protests and the police raids the protests evoked (including being tear-gassed and detained by the police) – he reportedly came to reject student strikes as a method of social change (Macey 1993: 209–31).

A notable point that is seldom mentioned in the literature is that Foucault chose to not get involved with labour-related issues, which were then at the top of the progressive agenda – in France especially but also in other countries. Foucault's avoidance of class politics was predictable: supporting trade unions and advancing workers' rights would have necessitated playing second fiddle to Jean-Paul Sartre; and would have required making a clear choice between the French Communist Party, the Maoists and the Trotskyists, and then following the 'discipline' of whichever leftist party or grouping was chosen.

Foucault did make some forays into the struggles then subsumed under the banner of anti-imperialism, in part because, having lived in Tunisia for a few years (which had the unintended effect of making him miss the famous Paris uprisings of May 1968), he was very conscious of French anti-Arab and anti-African racism. He actively participated in demonstrations and campaigns to protect immigrant rights. In participating in anti-racist and pro-immigrant activism, however, Foucault (along with other white left-wing Parisian intellectuals) promoted human rights and denounced discrimination and anti-immigrant policies, but without deeply entering into critiques of intellectual Eurocentrism. It is important for readers today to appreciate that, around 1970, terms like 'post-colonialism' or 'Orientalism' had not yet been coined. As Ann Stoler pointed out in an sympathetic but deep critique, Foucault shared the left's anti-imperialism, but seems not to have known much about the work of Frantz Fanon and the handful of writers from the Caribbean, North Africa, and elsewhere who were raising deep questions about white European intellectuals' taken-for-granted authority to speak on behalf of and about 'humanity'. Stoler, one of the first specialists on colonial rule to carefully evaluate the extent to which Foucault's work engages with and is useful for postcolonial studies, wrote that Foucault was:

> not the only one who failed to enlist the French intellectual left to take on these issues – nor is it clear that such a task would have been his intent. Although opposed to the wars in Indochina and Algeria, there is no indication that Foucault sought to situate his analysis of racism with respect to these political interventions ... While Albert Memmi, Frantz Fanon and Jean-Paul Sartre were among those who explicitly addressed colonial racism, [even] they did not prompt a general theoretical engagement with racism nor a confrontation with the racial underpinnings of French society itself. The concept of class and the sorts of social transformations to which capitalism gave rise remained foundational in critical social and political theory; race and racial theory was not.
>
> (Stoler 1995: 22–3)

And if Foucault's work did not benefit as much as it might have from the anti-racist theorists who were then emerging, his relation or non-relation to the feminism of his day is equally problematic, though for some unexplained reason this lack of engagement is far less discussed amongst Foucault scholars than the postcolonial question (Stoler herself being a good example). Foucault was certainly aware of the budding feminist activism and feminist thought going on around him (for example, he knew the great feminist philosopher Hélène Cixous personally). But other than lending occasional support to the pro-choice on abortion campaign (just as he endorsed the work of grassroots movements fighting anti-immigrant racism), feminism was simply invisible to him, intellectually. This is a serious case of wilful blindness. The medicalization of women's bodies and women's minds was beginning to be a major topic for women's health activists and a subject in a few pioneering works (mainly on the history of women's bodies). The topic is obviously highly relevant to Foucault's interest in the governance of mental illness, desires, bodies, and sexuality. How Foucault's work on 'biopolitics' and the history of sexuality might have differed if he had bothered to take feminist scholarship seriously is a question that will be taken up in Chapter 3 on biopolitics. But, in setting the political context for *Discipline and Punish*, all that needs to be noted here is that while Foucault made occasional forays into gay rights venues and engaged on occasion with fledgling gay rights publications, often in a critical rather than celebratory manner, the then more intellectually developed field of feminist thought seemed to be of no interest to him, either to learn from or to critique.

If one were to take a charitable view, it could be argued that if Foucault's thinking was not as informed by feminist or anti-racist thought as it might have been, that was because his political passions were as particular, as idiosyncratic, as his intellectual work. In general, Foucault had only a marginal involvement in the issues attracting the most sustained support from the intelligentsia in the early 1970s (workers' rights, imperialism, immigration, gender oppression). The one political issue Foucault selected as deserving of his energy was imprisonment, an issue then visible to left-wing intellectuals only insofar as political dissidents (especially, in Paris, Maoist activists) came to be imprisoned. And once he picked his issue, he gave it his considerable energy. His biographer, David Macey, explains that just a couple of months after his inaugural lecture as research professor at the most prestigious institution in France, the Collège de France, 'the political platform and even the street replaced the lecturer's dais. Elegant and erudite essays on Bataille and Blanchot gave way to hastily drafted statements to the press … meeting after meeting, demonstration after demonstration, confrontation after confrontation' (Macey 1993: 257).

Joining an existing group would not have been Foucault's style, however. Thus, in 1971, along with his younger partner Daniel Defert, Foucault founded the Groupe d'Information sur les Prisons (GIP) (Brich 2008). Over the next two years, Foucault devoted a vast amount of energy to the struggle to inform the French public about the inhumane conditions prevailing in the country's prisons. Sometimes he used his own name to gain media interest; sometimes he experimented instead with using a pseudonym in an effort to not have his fame dominate the discussion and overshadow the prisoners' point of view. The dilemma about whether or not to use a name that was already somewhat famous to publicize the cause also prompted him to appear on a television talk show with a bag over his head, introduced by the host as an anonymous 'masked philosopher'; and on other occasions he used a thinly disguised pseudonym (Casadamont 2008).

As shown by the experiments with the use or non-use of his name and face, the question of how authority is claimed by public intellectuals mattered a great deal to Foucault. Frequently, he denounced intellectuals who assumed that expertise in philosophy meant one had the right to tell labour unions or the French Communist Party (then a very large, mainly working-class organization) what to do. Jean-Paul Sartre, whose name was then constantly in the public eye as supporting or leading political campaigns, was probably an intended target of some of these attacks, though names were rarely mentioned. (Louis Althusser, the philosopher with the most influence on the global Marxist intelligentsia of the day, was certainly as guilty as Sartre of what one could call the Parisian philosophers' fallacy; but Foucault had been personally tutored by Althusser for the gruelling national *agrégation* examinations and always retained affection for him, so no direct criticism was ever made.)

Rejecting the traditional French theory (shared by Sartre and Althusser) that intellectuals should expect to be granted a leadership role in social movements, Foucault's small group, the GIP, did not seek to propose new laws or generate policy recommendations. Rather, the group sought to help prisoners gain agency and voice (at a time when no outsiders were tolerated in French prisons) by disseminating information about the injustices going on behind the prison gates. Importantly, throughout the life of the GIP, Foucault refused to single out the 'good' political prisoners from the ordinary criminals. This was innovative, since the left was then concerned only with the imprisonment of political dissidents, not with incarceration as such.

Information about prison conditions was sought by locating and contacting prisoner family members, who were asked to smuggle in the GIP's prisoner survey during their visits, fill it out with their imprisoned relatives, and smuggle the completed papers back out. Public meetings were later held to communicate the information gleaned from prisoners – with Foucault carefully eschewing anything that might look like reformist suggestions to make prisons nicer and less embarrassing for the government. A speech given in the very early days of the GIP conveys Foucault's sense of his role:

> None of us can be sure of avoiding prison. Less so than ever, today. Police control over our day-to-day lives is becoming tighter … They tell us that the prisons are overpopulated. But what if it were the population that were overimprisoned? Little information is published about prisons; this is one of the hidden regions of our social system.
>
> (Macey 1993: 258)

Foucault's unaccustomed activist work is probably a major reason why *Discipline and Punish* was so long in the making – even after the Collège de France, from 1970 onward, provided Foucault with an ideal research environment. In the interests of recognizing the material conditions of thought, it should be noted that those who hold chairs in the Collège are not normal professors; their job description is limited to an annual series of public lectures. There are no regular courses or formal thesis supervision, since the Collège does not grant any degrees. Given this rather idyllic work situation, Foucault could have engaged in at least some activism while still doing a great deal of research and academic publishing. But perhaps combining activism with research in archives was not easy. It is important to note that Foucault, unlike many of his contemporaries, had previously had very little experience in grassroots activism. Not unrelatedly, it was during this activist phase of his life that Foucault's writing style underwent a very marked change, with philosophical discourse coming to be overshadowed by analyses of everyday practices of governance, and abstract denunciations of exclusion and vaguely anarchist odes to 'transgression' came to be replaced by research-based specific analyses of different forms of power-knowledge.

How and why the GIP petered out is not clearly established in the available literature. What is clear, however, in hindsight, is that a small, purely local group focused on generating data about prison conditions and disseminating that information by using the opportunities enjoyed by its middle-class intellectual members was not likely to have a long life, especially if engaging with state authorities to obtain small reforms was out of the question due to Foucault's consistently radical, anti-reformist stance.

There is a larger, global context for the GIP that may be worth outlining, since political action today tends to take more institutionalized forms (with notable exceptions, such as the Occupy movement of 2008–09). The 1970s was a decade in which activism flourished on a global scale in unprecedented ways. But independent grassroots groups such as GIP were by definition not sustained by a classic political party (as had been the case for the 'communist front' organizations and trade unions of the 1950s and 1960s); and, more significantly, neither were these usually strictly local groups sustained by a stable national or global non-governmental organization (NGO). It is thus not surprising that most of the 1970s 'collectives' came to an end after a few years of often frantic activity (some with a bang and others with a whimper). This was a worldwide phenomenon, marking a clear break, in organizational terms, between the 'Old' (communist and socialist) Left and the 'New Left'. Lacking support in ongoing traditional political or NGO structures, New Left groups were notoriously fragile. In the US, for example, the Black Panthers in the early 1970s were doing a great deal to expose mistreatment and racism in prisons such as Angola, Louisiana and Attica, New York; but their embrace of armed struggle enabled state authorities to simply imprison or even kill them, and cut off potential support from less radical groups. And other grassroots groups were equally ephemeral, albeit for different reasons.

In general, the New Left of the 1970s had big new ideas about collectivity and consensus, with activists being always quick to denounce the bureaucratic and undemocratic habits of the Old Left; but the New Left notoriously lacked organizational capacity and collective stamina. If I can insert a personal note to illustrate this point: after being active in the left-wing sector of the Toronto women's movement for a few hectic years (1977–85), based primarily in a socialist-feminist collective that participated in or led myriad often difficult coalitions, I came to realize the great wisdom of a pamphlet whose title perfectly described the organizational flaw of the New Left, including my own group – 'The tyranny of structurelessness'. Anything like a formal group structure with presidents and vice-presidents would have been anathema to most of my friends of the time; that was also the case for Foucault, who always kept his distance not only from the French Communist Party but also from the more radical Gauche Prolétarienne (GP). But without a clear and long-lasting structure, a group will either die out for lack of care and sustenance, or will self-destruct in polemics that cannot be settled because there is no acknowledged procedure to resolve disputes, and nobody is authorized to adjudicate conflicts.

Given this larger transnational New Left context, the GIP can be understood as a two-fold project. First, it was a practical result of Foucault's rejection of the French tradition of intellectuals pontificating to activists and practitioners, and of his related decision to practise a more humble style of intellectual leadership by working on an issue that the rest of the left neglected (imprisonment). Second, the GIP was also a good example of the anti-establishment, anti-reformist New Left groups that bubbled up all over the world at the time but that could not possibly have had a long life, given the poor 'networking' and institutional capacities of New Left local groups.

We have lingered over the political context of *Discipline and Punish* more than most commentators do because few Foucaultian criminologists today appreciate the broader political context. But it is now finally time to turn to the text of the book – always keeping in mind that, of all of Foucault's works (including not only the books but also the posthumously published lectures), *Discipline and Punish* was unusual in its deep connection with activism.

Contrasting 'penal styles'

Foucault's most famous book opens not with a normal book introduction but with an unnecessarily lengthy, almost pornographic description of the kind of eighteenth-century judicial torture that Voltaire famously denounced. Even readers already familiar with Voltaire's and Cesare Beccaria's denunciations of legalized state violence, which themselves verged on torture porn, are likely to be jolted by the description (from a contemporary document) of how a man found guilty of the crime of regicide, in 1757, was ritually tortured and executed. First the prisoner's body was literally broken on that barbaric European invention, the wheel; then the executioner wielded muscle-tearing metal instruments and poured molten metal into the wounds; eventually, the body was literally torn limb from limb (with a great deal of trouble on the part of the four horses involved) and the body parts burned – with the ashes finally scattered so as to efface all traces of the criminal.

The reader is then taken, without pause for breath or explanation, to a youth reformatory 'eighty years later' – or rather, not the reformatory itself, but only its official schedule. The youthful inmates were probably beaten and mistreated at least occasionally, if the reformatory in question was at all typical; but by making the rigid but very explicitly non-violent schedule stand for the whole institution, Foucault achieves a perfect, clean contrast between two 'penal style[s]' (Foucault 1979).

Foucault's choice of opening vignettes appears at first sight to replicate Beccaria's famous project to reform criminal law and criminal justice. As is well known, Beccaria wanted to 'humanize' punishment by abolishing public executions, torture, and physical punishment; but humanization was for him not just morally worthy. Abolishing practices that caused bodily pain was also a means to larger political end, namely, creating legal institutions and practices that would act on the soul and mind, not the body. Beccaria's vision sought to institute new 'enlightened' practices that would cultivate habits of disciplined labour and non-violent, future-oriented thought amongst offenders; and at the same time cultivate humane, civilized sensibilities among the general public. For both Beccaria and his enlightened contemporaries (Voltaire, for example) the protracted, cruel execution of people like Foucault's example, Robert-François Damiens (which to make things worse took place in public), was not only an extreme example of state barbarism against a citizen, but arguably had barbaric effects upon the law-abiding public as well. As against this, the reformatory's schedule seems like the height of civilization and improvement.

But, contrary to Enlightenment popular belief – and contrary to the self-congratulatory discourse of the late eighteenth-century reformers who sought to eliminate public displays of physical punishment – in Foucault's account 'the disappearance of torture as a public spectacle' (Foucault 1979: 7) turns out to lead not to liberty, civilization, refined sensibilities and equality, but rather to a more subtle form of state violence and control. Violence becomes structural and silent, and is rarely used by one person against the body of another. Punishment in modern criminal justice is not about causing pain, but rather about depriving offenders of that which the Enlightenment and the French Revolution valued more than life itself – that is, liberty – while attempting to reform and rehabilitate the prisoner. Thus, 'from being an art of unbearable sensations punishment has become an economy of suspended rights' (ibid.: 11).

And if eliminating direct physical pain in favour of long-term 'correctional' discipline is a key part of the shift that created modern penality, so too was removing punishment from public view an equally important strategy for the development of modern criminal justice. Whipping people in public squares or exposing them to ridicule in stocks – and, especially, hanging people in full public view – were techniques for governing criminality that acted as much or more on the public than on the offender. And in relation to the public, displays of painful punishments told citizens that breaches of 'the King's peace' would not be tolerated, and that sovereign power will sooner or later be restored to its previous, pre-crime terrible majesty.

The second element (turning punishment into a private event rather than a public spectacle) would seem to have been more successfully implemented than the first (shifting from punishing offences through bodily pain to acting on the soul or self). Foucault points out that even the most enlightened correctional institutions, after all, act on bodies, quite directly, by limiting food and fresh air; allowing only regimented, slow walking around a courtyard instead of free movement; imposing a drab uniform, shaving heads, and resorting to measures such as sleep deprivation and bread and water diets (Foucault 1979: 16). But these less obviously painful measures to regiment and constrain the body came to be almost universally conducted out of public view, within the walls of an institution. And what Foucault does not state explicitly but is implied (especially if one knows about his prison activism), as the twentieth century wore on, imprisonment, whether expanding or contracting in volume, still remained out of public view. Occasionally, a rash of deaths in custody or other events might cause a short-lived scandal to emerge; but for the most part, throughout the West, citizens' ideas about their own country's prisons came to be derived mainly from American fictional films and television series rather than from any knowledge of actual institutions.

Within the walls of the institutions, Foucault was not primarily interested in the persistence of physical punishment despite the claims about humanness, or in riots and protests by prisoners, how prisoners got along or fought with one another, or in any other empirically important feature. What interested Foucault was a theoretical point: that the rise of the rigidly disciplined (ideal) penitentiary and its prestige and popularity indicates a larger shift in governance. The pages of *Discipline and Punish* contain almost no accounts of prison escapes, riots, guard murders, and so on. But the 'Where is prisoners' agency?' lament that progressive criminology students reading Foucault often voice is based on a misperception of Foucault's goal. His goal was not to produce an accurate social history of imprisonment in France, but rather to map and analyse what later Foucaultian scholars would call the more general 'diagrams of power' that, in often less coercive or visible forms, spread throughout modern societies. The governance of the unfree, in other words, is seen by Foucault as a kind of pilot project foreshadowing how whole populations would come to be controlled – or, more accurately, how various authorities would come to imagine that 'free' populations ought to be monitored, disciplined, and controlled, since control outside prison walls can never be as far-reaching as control within the prison.

The key analytical tool used for this theoretical purpose is the contrast drawn between the 'two penal styles' described in such stark terms in the first part of the book. The older, 'sovereign' penal style relied on public hangings as well as other public displays of royal majesty and honour. The new, 'disciplinary' style, by contrast, preferred indoor locations and was marked by a drab rather than a majestic aesthetic – the abandonment of spectacle and terror in favour of constant supervision and monitoring.

In the 1973 lectures at the College de France, Foucault boldly stated that:

> this is precisely what takes place in the modern epoch: this inversion of the spectacle into surveillance. We are in the process [in the 1820s] of inventing ... not just an architecture, an urbanism, but a whole mental disposition in general.
>
> (Foucault 2015: 23)

Instead of the many gathering to watch spectacles – from royal coronations to public executions (the many watching the one) – as disciplining populations and socializing individuals come to replace the mere defence of the sovereign's honour, the few are employed to watch the many. Early nineteenth-century prisons were the great laboratory in which techniques for having very few people employed watching the many efficiently were first developed.

And indeed, the surveillant gaze perfected in early nineteenth-century penitentiaries was adopted by one organization after another: factories, schools, even playgrounds. Eventually (as direct, embodied supervision gave way to CCTV), this way of governing by supervision spread to shops, banks, train stations, and even streets and squares, thus colonizing in a complete and continuous manner the public spaces that had previously only seen sporadic spectacles of sovereignty and punishment.

In some passages of *Discipline and Punish* the dissemination of disciplinary techniques of surveillance is described in an almost deterministic manner, as if modern societies inevitably had to develop this type of gaze. But even in the published book –

which presents a pared-down, rather simplified account (compared to the various lecture series covering some of the same topics, which abound in subplots left out of the book) – there is a relatively detailed consideration of the historical contingency of the penitentiary as the preferred technique for punishing offenders. The second part of *Discipline and Punish*, one often skipped by criminology instructors (including the present writer) as well as students, is devoted to describing a variety of experiments in penality that did not seek to remove punishment wholly out of public view, but rather sought to utilize 'humane' and crime-specific punishment to educate the general public. Considering this neglected part of the book, however briefly, will help demonstrate that if parts of Foucault's account of the rise of 'discipline' can be faulted for being somewhat determinist, his account of the history of punishment is certainly not.

The civilized punitive city: the road not taken

As Foucault notes, the ideas about criminal justice in a civilized, enlightened society that Beccaria and other late eighteenth-century criminal-law reformers disseminated sounded good in theory, but were very difficult to translate into criminal law statutes and criminal justice policies. Beccaria exhorted monarchs and parliamentarians to throw out the discredited 'bloody codes', with their excess of cruelty, and put in place instead a civilized system whereby the penalty exacted for each crime would impose just enough pain and suffering to deter that particular crime, and no more. But how exactly could criminal codes implement the theory that offenders should be regarded as rational-choice individuals (whether they actually are or not, in the individual case); and, to make things more difficult, the complementary theory that society would inevitably become more civilized if the criminal justice system became a model of rationality, fairness, and moderation?

In the chapter 'Generalized Punishment', Foucault notes that at the time when Beccaria and others were working to create a rational criminal code that would treat everyone exactly the same – specifically, as a disembodied rational choice subject – there was also a growing sense that human beings are not all the same, and do not all respond to stimuli in the same manner. Individualization of punishment was a project in keeping with the rise of modern scientific and medical knowledge of the mind; but individualizing punishment is a notion that is quite at odds with the great rationalist dream of imposing the rule of law, abolishing special aristocratic and clerical judicial systems, and creating a written code that would apply to all equally (Foucault 1979: 96–97). Rationalist legal reform (including codification) is based on the Enlightenment idea that reason is what matters in humans, and that all human beings are therefore equal – not in fact but for legal purposes. Rationalist codification could therefore include individual factors only in a secondary way, for example, as 'mitigating factors' in sentencing hearings. But despite this tension with codification, a number of experiments in trying to fit not just the punishment to the crime but also the punishment to the offender were carried out in different European jurisdictions (ibid.: 99–100).

Oddly, Foucault does not himself explain the significance of the various projects that attempted to individualize punishment. In order to do so, he could easily have referred back to or borrowed from his earlier work on the history of psychiatry; but for some reason he decided to keep the account in *Discipline and Punish* as wholly autonomous and self-contained. The comments about 'individualization' in criminal-law reform in this part of the book thus remain rather cryptic. In particular, the comments in Part II of the book ('Punishment') are not linked to the argument made later in the book about how law in general (which later in the book is conflated with sovereign modes of power, and is not seen as having any internal interest in individualization) comes to be overshadowed by expert-generated norms.

If some of the undeveloped comments in these two chapters suggest that individualization is perhaps not as external to law's logic as the later, much better known chapters declare, so too the somewhat simplistic claim that public spectacles of punishment came to be replaced, completely, by closed institutions is qualified in the chapter 'The Gentle Way in Punishment'. This describes a variety of experiments in using criminal punishment to both reform offenders and educate and civilize the population, experiments that often involved the public display of the (now rationalized) punishment process. A common tactic, one clearly connected to the need of industrializing nations to turn peasants into wage labourers, involved ordering offenders to perform forced labour, either inside prisons themselves or in public works such as highways.

Since prison labour designed to produce market commodities has the potential to undermine private enterprise, forced public works labour – which does not undermine private capitalists but rather supports their profit-making endeavours – has at various times been seen as the obvious solution to the problem of crime: it creates factory-style habits among the lower orders and at the same time produces publicly funded infrastructure, a great need of early capitalism. From the capitalist point of view, therefore, the 'chain gangs' that persisted in the US South well into the twentieth century would seem a more appropriate, more economically sound method of punishment than imprisonment.

But the political economy of chain-gang solutions is not what Foucault stresses. Instead, he highlights the symbolic and political dimensions of prisoner labour programmes (perhaps because the reformers advocating them were not usually trying to make economic arguments). Drawing on a variety of sources, Foucault synthesizes various proposals and experiments that would reform prisoners, provide rational punishment, and educate the populace all at the same time, through what Foucault calls 'the punitive city':

> This is, then, how one must imagine the punitive city. At the crossroads, in the gardens, at the side of roads being repaired or bridges built, in workshops open to all, in the depths of mines that may be visited, will be hundreds of tiny theatres of punishment.
>
> (Foucault 1979: 113)

To stress the link between particular offenders, particular crimes, and specific, rationally justifiable punishments not only will different kinds of labour be assigned to different prisoners, but also the convicts themselves will become walking advertisements of the rationality of the system: 'placards, different-coloured caps bearing inscriptions, posters, symbols' (Foucault 1979: 113).

> Around each of these 'moral representations', schoolchildren will gather with their masters and adults will learn what lessons to teach their offspring. The great terrifying ritual of the public execution gives way, day after day, street after street, to this serious theatre.
>
> (Foucault 1979: 113)

These experiments in shaming convicts while edifying the public – experiments that if widely adopted might have put penitentiary confinement in the background – did not take hold, however, at least not in Western Europe. Without mentioning the varied and often not particularly civilized modes of punishment being practised in colonies, including those of the French empire, Foucault, having described several experiments in using punishment as educational theatre, simply states that 'within a short space of time, detention became the essential form of punishment' (Foucault 1979: 115).

The 'punitive city', the city that was supposed to be dotted with public displays of moderate and rationally justified punishment, did not prosper, according to Foucault. A critical reader might point out that the Chinese cultural revolution's massive use of public shaming and forced labour in the 1960s shows that the punitive city ideal could be not only resuscitated but even rescaled at the state level – but such a comment would have detracted from the elegance, simplicity and neatness of *Discipline and Punish* and its two penal styles. As suggested earlier, Foucault did not aim to provide either a sociology or a history of punishment; rather, he sought to map certain diagrams of power/knowledge in a stark and memorable fashion. The punitive city thus makes a cameo appearance only as a counterfactual, as an approach that did not prosper, historically. This was perhaps unfortunate. Elsewhere in the book, the term 'to punish' is taken as referring to the measures taken by sovereign powers to protect their authority and honour, with most of the modern punishments that go on in penitentiaries being classified under the banner of 'to discipline'. This binary opposition of sovereignty vs. discipline, punishment vs. surveillance is partially deconstructed in the brief accounts of the punitive city projects – projects which readily combined rationality and bodily constraint, legal equality and correctional differentiation, punishment and discipline, sovereignty and individualized surveillance. We will return, in the final section of the chapter, to the question of whether the sharp contrast between the two penal styles that is laid out in the initial chapter of *Discipline and Punish* and developed at length in Part III thereof is best taken as a heuristic device that does not map directly onto criminal justice reality. But first it is necessary to briefly go over the features of the second penal style – that known in English as 'discipline' – which, as we know, is characterized by monitoring, supervision, and micromanaged individual conduct.

The birth of the prison

Modern penitentiaries, even if they abolished whipping and other harsh physical punishments, certainly acted on bodies as well as souls, non-violently but intrusively – as is explained at length in the chapter 'Docile bodies'. This part of the book opens with detailed descriptions not of prisons but of military drill. The theoretical point being made here is that even if penitentiaries are important laboratories of modern governance, the criminal justice system is not a self-contained sphere whose history can be narrated separately from that of other institutions using similar methods and having similar governing effects. As against the tendency of criminologists and criminal justice historians to isolate the realm of penality, then, Foucault stresses the importance of national armies in the development of techniques for governing large numbers of men while avoiding possible chaos or resistance by inventing tactics ensuring the standardization of the appearance and the conduct of the human beings in question. Many of the drill exercises used to train early modern armies may well have been useless or even disadvantageous in actual battle; but rigidly micromanaging every step, every glance, every button and buckle, and every bit of hair (as armies did then and still do now) is a tactic that effectively promoted the larger purpose of training future citizens in states that, in the early days of industrialization, required a great deal of blind obedience and a great deal of very tedious, standardized, rigidly controlled factory work.

In this chapter Foucault also highlights the important role played by monasteries and religious orders generally in the habituation of large sections of the population to obedience, regimentation, bodily restraint, and uniformity of physical appearance. It was medieval religious institutions that invented 'the cell', that key architectural technology of modern prisons. And it was religious institutions that, even before clocks were invented, were 'the specialists of time, the great technicians of rhythm and regular activity' (Foucault 1979: 115). The religious day was divided into uniform chunks of time marked by time-specific services (matins, compline, etc.) – unlike the working day of the peasantry, whose temporal divides varied greatly by season.

The cell and the clock, therefore, were not invented (as a Marxist might think) by the factories of early industrialism; they were invented well before industrial capitalism by institutions that required temporal standardization and uniformity of behaviour for quite different, spiritual reasons. And similar techniques for dividing up space and time in standard chunks, for enforcing bodily uniformity, and for arranging human beings in ordered, symmetrical rows were also developed, somewhat later, by seventeenth- and eighteenth-century armies, as mentioned before – during a time when factories did not yet exist. This historical fact illustrates a general methodological point rooted in Nietzsche's radical critique of the functionalist fallacy, that critique amounting to pointing out that the historical origins of particular techniques of governance says little or nothing about the uses to which those techniques might be put at later times or in other places.

If Foucault, learning from Nietzsche, does not believe that identifying actual historical origins allows us to know the 'essence' of a particular invention or technique, then what is the significance of the long descriptions of the micromanagement ambitions of both military and religious authorities in the century or two before industrial capitalism? Foucault's decision to linger at length on pre-industrial pioneers of human discipline has two important implications. First, the penitentiary now appears a lot less original than its inventors claimed. Whether or not the penitentiary promoters knew anything about medieval monasteries or seventeenth-century armies, they borrowed a whole array of techniques from these institutions – from the idea that prisoners should wear uniforms, to the architectural devices and timetables used to isolate convicts and force them to reflect on their crimes. This illustrates a larger point, one that Foucault does not explicitly make in this book but that is found scattered throughout his work: that particular techniques for governing humans and things through space and through time are constantly borrowed and adapted for new uses across institutions. It is therefore problematic to write 'histories of the prison' or 'histories of the mental hospital', as if these types of institution emerged from scratch and had distinct and separate histories.

A larger point is that if institutions of control and discipline are not self-contained, designed from scratch and tailor-made, but are rather assemblages of borrowed techniques, so too the knowledges that develop within and out of these institutions (e.g. psychiatry, in the case of asylums, or criminology, in the case of prisons) are perhaps not as self-contained as their respective practitioners might like to think. Today, criminologists are well aware of the fact that many techniques used in correctional contexts do not have a criminological origin, but are rather borrowed from other realms (as is the case with correctional 'risk management' tools and prediction models). The spread of psychometric techniques and methods to the correctional realm has been seen by some as exceptional, as caused by neoliberalism or some other recent trend. But Foucault's research on the history of disciplinary techniques – and indeed his work on other topics, such as the history of neoliberal economics (Foucault 2008) – suggests that cross-institutional flows of knowledges and ways of governing are not the exception, but are rather the rule. And the implication which in turn arises from this point is that the very idea of writing or teaching the history of criminal justice or the history of criminology is problematic. The subtitle of *Discipline and Punish* is 'the *birth* of the prison' because a great deal of time is devoted to explaining how pre-industrial techniques and devices were put together, in the early nineteenth century, to form a novel network (the penitentiary). The subtitle is not 'the *history* of the prison'.

Observation, examination, normalization

'The Means of Correct Training' is the one chapter of this book that I have consistently used as a text for my Foucault classes. Other sections of the book, and other parts of other books, come and go in my course syllabus, but this one is never absent.

The first section of the chapter is entitled 'hierarchical observation'. This term covers an array of techniques for supervising or monitoring groups of people either by direct visual observation or by arranging buildings and objects in such a way as to allow and foster surveillance by authorities – the techniques used in 'working-class housing estates, hospitals, asylums, prisons, schools' that Foucault says amount to 'the spatial nesting of hierarchized surveillance' (Foucault 1979: 171–2). Hierarchical observation reaches its peak in Jeremy Bentham's invention, which he called the 'panopticon', from Greek words meaning 'seeing all'. The panopticon was a central observation tower from which a single prison guard could observe all the corridors and even the cells of a prison; this watchtower was to be constructed in such a way as to make prisoners feel that they were being watched even when the guard was not on duty. This is familiar to us today – the panopticon notion is the principle behind the sign reading 'This area is under CCTV surveillance', a sign meant to deter and prevent unruly conduct even when nobody is watching the footage.

Apart from perfect one-guard or zero-guard panopticons, which are not very common either in prison life or in other institutions, there are many less perfectly designed situations in which 'hierarchical observation' is an appropriate descriptor of the mode of power/knowledge at work. The humble schoolteacher's raised dais, for example, is built in such a way that the teacher can see at least part of the students' body and much or all of their papers and books. Elsewhere, the factory manager's glass-walled office, situated well above the shop floor, also enables hierarchical observation, and acts as a message, for the workers, that management could always be watching, even if nobody is in fact watching. But what is the purpose, the aim, and the effect of all of this watching activity?

In the 'docile bodies' chapter, as seen above, the emphasis is on uniformity and conformity. In the army, in the monastery and in many schools, everyone wears the same clothes, moves at the same time, and even has the same knowledge and the same values. However, what is probably the most innovative aspect of Foucault's thinking about discipline is that he notes that conformity and uniformity are not in fact the opposite of individualization. The monk whose clothes, meals, prayer times and bedtimes are rigidly regimented has a rich, individual spiritual relationship with God that is not exactly the same as that of other monks; the pursuit of sainthood is highly personal. So too, the penitentiary was not meant as some kind of fascist training camp. The penitentiary was made up of techniques that simultaneously produced conformity and individualization. How?

A technique of governance that, once again, did not originate in the prison system itself is said by Foucault to be the key means for reconciling uniformity and individualization: the examination. This term has at least two meanings in Foucault's work on discipline. The first refers to the examinations that students sit in school and that generate grades that enable the institution to rank students, thus enabling them to know how they stand, as individuals, against others. The examination – or more exactly the evaluation or grading that is the real purpose of the examination – thus generates individual results and, as the results of different examinations in the same institution are compiled in a student's file, individual profiles. But at the same time, once statistical methods develop, the results are used to represent the total population and show its distribution graphically on a curve, usually a normal curve. Students can thus feel individualized – and indeed *are* individualized – as they find out that they are 'A' students or 'C' students; that they are good at maths but not so good at languages, etc. As Foucault writes, 'the examination, surrounded by all its documentary techniques, makes each individual a "case"' (1979: 191). But at the same time that individuals with certain distinctive qualities and capacities emerge, authorities gain knowledge of the school itself, the school as a population with certain features. Authorities at a level higher than that of the individual school can do to schools in their area what the school does to students: that is, create a 'profile' based on a number of examination results. The school too can become 'a case', as we see when certain public (state) schools are 'diagnosed' as needing to be turned into academies that are governed as if they were private (independent) schools. The production of school league tables, therefore, is a current practice that illustrates how the same tools that are used to differentiate individual students from one another can also be used, without any additional work, to compare schools (that is, school-based populations) with one another, generating a bureaucracy of 'case files' in which the 'case' is the school rather than the individual.

Examination, however, is hardly monopolized by schools. It is a flexible technique found in other forms. In particular, physicians have long performed examinations, physical and mental. Taking up the subject position of 'patient' means subjecting oneself to examinations (and, these days, physical tests as well, where the object scrutinized is not the body as a whole but rather microprocesses such as blood pressure, cholesterol levels, etc.). Premodern medicine used generic classifications for patients – using the four humours, for example; but modern medicine developed more fine-grained categories, especially in regard to troubles of the mind.

A key point here is that, in keeping with the general approach to studying power and knowledge explained in Chapter 1, Foucault is not stating that modern techniques for governing people are better able to see and identify individuals. Such a way of speaking would assume that individuals exist, prior to being governed – that is, it would assume the liberal theory of prepolitical individuality trumpeted by liberal legal and political thinkers since Hobbes. Foucault is saying instead that 'individuality' does not exist in any sort of state of nature, but is in fact the product, the effect, of certain ways of governing people. Examinations, observation, and normalization (as when individual test results are arranged along a curve) produce the modern individual, who defines him- or herself against others by means of the kind of data also used by authorities to govern populations.

If I can use an anecdote from my own childhood, when IQ tests were administered in my high school, we were not told what our overall score was but we were told how we did in respect to our fellow students. Knowing that my language skills, as measured by the test, were better than those of 100 per cent of my colleagues (so that my score was literally off the chart) became an important part of my self-identity – although I knew very well that the main reason for my high score was that, having been brought up speaking and writing Spanish, I could easily discern/guess the meaning of many obscure English words of Latin origin that stumped my unilingual Anglophone friends. My mathematical skills, which were very good as measured by regular school examinations, were by contrast said to be relatively poor in the IQ test. Asking my teacher what had gone wrong, we ascertained that at one point I had turned over two pages of the test at once, so that two whole pages were accidentally left blank. As in the case of the quite accidental supergifted language score, I knew how contingent and arguably invalid the lower maths score on the IQ test was; but, nevertheless, both my teachers and I persisted in labelling me as suited to writing essays rather than to doing math problems, at a time when such identifications had life-long consequences.

Thus, as Foucault writes:

> [T]he examination is at the centre of the procedures that constitute the individual as effect and object of power, as effect and object of knowledge. It is the examination which, by combining hierarchical surveillance and normalizing judgement, assures the great disciplinary functions of distribution and classification … [and the] optimum combination of aptitudes [hence creating 'individuality' itself].
>
> (Foucault 1979: 192)

Liberal legal and political theory, as is well known, assumes that autonomous individuals have always existed, and that their individuality and their choice to give up part of their natural-born freedom to form a government are the foundation of politics and law. For Foucault, however, the autonomous individual is a product of certain practices of governance.

The notion that the autonomous individual is made rather than born was not unique. Althusser's key contribution to Marxism was precisely to argue that bourgeois ideology brings the liberal autonomous subject into being while covering its own traces, such that the sovereign individual appears as existing since time immemorial. Foucault adopts the general idea, but removes it from the class-based model of power. For Foucault individuality is created not only by bourgeois ideology but also by a wide range of modern techniques of governance, from school examinations to correctional practices to 'surveillance' of different kinds:

> The individual is no doubt the fictitious atom of an 'ideological' representation of society; but he is also a reality fabricated by this specific technology of power that I have called 'discipline'. We must cease once and for all to describe the effects of power in negative terms ... In fact, power produces; it produces reality; it produces domains of objects and rituals of truth. The individual and the knowledge that may be gained of him belong to this production.
>
> (Foucault 1979: 194)

In *Discipline and Punish* the argument about the creation of the individual – and the myth that the individual has always existed – has a somewhat Marxist flavour, as Foucault stresses how industrial capitalism needed a disciplined labour force that bought the myth that we are the masters of our own fate. Later on, in other work, the Marxist argument about labour and industry would recede into the background. In later chapters we will explore other Foucaultian texts that describe the ways in which some forms of power, rather than suppressing individuality, incite it or even bring it into being – an insight that became, in the 1990s, the foundation of the vast literature known as 'governmentality studies'. But for now enough has been said to alert readers that while *Discipline and Punish* sometimes sounds a little like Orwell's *1984*, there is a crucial difference. For Foucault control and discipline do not work against individuality, but rather help create the very individual that then tries to pursue his/her freedom. This of course means that 'freedom' is not as simple as dethroning the tyrant and speaking up or rebelling, as an individual. But freedom is not a topic considered in *Discipline and Punish*, so it will be left to later chapters.

Panopticism

Few prisons built in the nineteenth century, or at any other time, actually implemented the panopticon idea put forward by Jeremy Bentham. But Bentham's plan nevertheless exemplified the disciplinary idea, and is thus discussed at some length in what may be the most famous pages ever written by Foucault.

Older prisons and gaols featured masses of people, usually thrown together in large rooms where they constantly interacted with one another and with their gaolers. The modern penitentiary, with its isolated prisoners confined to cells and watched by guards they cannot themselves see, is not, therefore, an offshoot of the old local gaol. Instead, it is an improvement (so to speak) on the plague hospitals that were built in European cities in the 1600s and 1700s. The medical control exercised over those who either had the plague or were suspected of harbouring it in their bodies was modified and raised to a new level in Bentham's famous panopticon, a building in which surveillance could take place very efficiently from a central location – a building in which inmates were separated from each other but were also rendered unable to see, much less speak with, their guards. If a single guard could occupy a central tower from which he could see into cells and corridors without himself being seen, prisoners would feel the surveillance even if the guard was asleep or absent (just as a CCTV camera has an effect on passersby even if it is not actually working):

> Hence the major effect of the Panopticon: to induce in the inmate a state of conscious and permanent visibility that

> assures the automatic functioning of power … [T]his architectural apparatus [is] a machine for creating and sustaining a power relation independent of the person who exercises it.
> (Foucault 1979: 201)

The panopticon thus depersonalizes observation and discipline – while rendering the watched inmate hyperconscious of his or her own conduct. It is thus a great invention if one wants to exercise great power in a silent, impersonal, and almost automatic manner – in such a way as to constantly push those observed to behave properly. And it is perhaps the panopticon that is the best example of the point made at the outset of the chapter about how prison techniques were important for Foucault not because he thinks prisons are fascinating, but because prisons were the laboratories of modern governance. Thus, as we know from our own daily experience with CCTV and other forms of surveillance, 'the panoptic scheme, without disappearing as such or losing any of its properties, was destined to spread throughout the social body' (Foucault 1979: 207).

This chapter has described the key components of Foucault's notion of 'discipline', focusing on explaining why the penitentiary, although the main research site for Foucault's work, was not in fact the object of his analysis: the reason his work is widely known and used well beyond criminology is precisely that the ideas associated with the term 'discipline' apply to all manner of everyday activities and contexts. In the next chapter we will go on to a different term that has also been used in a very wide variety of contemporary studies – less perhaps within criminology, but certainly within legal studies, especially studies involving colonial or neo-colonial governance. That term is 'biopolitics'.

Notes

1 Without mentioning Sheridan's translator's choice, Graham Burchell explains in his translator's note to the Collège de France 1972–73 lectures *The Punitive Society* (which includes much of the material published in the 1975 book) that he decided to use a variety of English words to translate the diverse meanings of the French verb *surveiller* and the noun *surveillance*. These terms, Burchell points out, include 'supervision', 'monitoring' and 'watching over'. To me, Burchell's

approach to translating *surveiller* seems to be in keeping with my comments here, although he may or may not agree. See Foucault (2015).

2 The earlier books were rhetorically closer to the norms of philosophy and high literature; but from the 1970s onward Foucault's publications and lectures were filled with commentaries on texts selected from archives rather than from high culture, accompanied by minimal overtly theoretical conclusions. Most notably, volumes II and III of the *History of Sexuality*, the last books to appear in Foucault's lifetime, consist largely of commentaries on minor Greek, Roman, and early Christian texts (for example, Aristotle is mentioned only in regard to his advice on eating and everyday ethics, his metaphysics going unmentioned). Without the name on the cover, one would never know that these two modest, slim volumes were written by the author of *The Order of Things*. The very marked, indeed drastic change that took place in the early 1970s in Foucault's writing style (which has few if any parallels amongst major theorists) has not been noted, much less discussed, by social scientists or legal scholars who use his work.

3 French social historians were very unhappy with Foucault's approach to writing the history of French criminal justice (see Macey 1993: 402).

Bibliography

Brich, Cecile. 2008. 'The Group d'information sur les prisons: the voice of prisoners? Or Foucault's?', *Foucault Studies* 5: 26–47.

Casadamont, Guy. 2008. 'Masques de Foucault', in Bernard Harcourt, ed., *Carceral Notebooks, Volume 4: Discipline, Security, and Beyond: Rethinking Michel Foucault's 1978 and 1979 Collège de France Lectures*. Chicago, IL: B. Harcourt, pp. 45–53. Also available at www.thecarceral.org/journal-vol4.html.

Foucault, Michel. 1979. *Discipline and Punish: The Birth of the Prison*. Translated by Alan Sheridan. New York: Vintage Books.

Foucault, Michel. 2008. *The Birth of Biopolitics: Lectures at the Collège de France, 1978–1979*. Edited by Michel Senellart. Translated by Graham Burchell. New York: Picador.

Foucault, Michel. 2015. *The Punitive Society: Lectures at the Collège de France 1972–1973*. Edited by Bernard E. Harcourt. Translated by Graham Burchell. Basingstoke: Palgrave Macmillan.

Geertz, Clifford. 1978. 'Stir Crazy', *New York Review of Books*, January 26. Available at http://www.nybooks.com/articles/1978/01/26/stir-crazy.

Macey, David. 1993. *The Lives of Michel Foucault*. London: Hutchinson.

Stoler, Ann Laura. 1995. *Race and the Education of Desire: Foucault's History of Sexuality and the Colonial Order of Things*. Durham, NC: Duke University Press.

Chapter 3

Biopolitics

The neologism 'biopolitics' has now become such a common term in critical social science that it no longer requires a footnote. The term emerged into public view in print in the final section of *The History of Sexuality Vol. I: An Introduction* (Foucault 1980).[1] This slim volume, which many people (including the present writer) consider the most significant and innovative work published in Foucault's lifetime, was translated into English in 1978. It originally appeared in French in 1976 under the title *La Volonte de Savoir* (*The Will to Know*) – a phrase referencing Nietzsche's famous 'will to power'. The section in question begins as follows:

> For a long time, one of the characteristic privileges of sovereign power was the right to decide life and death. In a formal sense, it derived no doubt from the ancient *patria potestas* that granted the father of the Roman family the right to 'dispose' of the life of his children and his slaves.
>
> (Foucault 1980: 135)

The Roman patriarchal power to dispose of the life of the members of one's household was used as both a metaphor and more than a metaphor later on by European kings seeking to justify their claims to monopolize legal power in their kingdoms, imagined as large-scale households. But this power evolved and became subject to certain rules and norms. In order to justify sovereignty as distinct from arbitrary tyranny, 'the power of life and death was not an absolute privilege: it was conditioned by the defense of the sovereign, and his own survival' (ibid.). A relevant example here would be the Tudor monarchs in Britain, who executed anyone who rose against them or was even suspected of plotting, including many close relatives; but they did so only after formal charges of treason had been articulated and prosecuted. This contrasts with the intra-family murders that characterized the late Roman Empire, most of which were assassinations rather than executions since there was no pretence even of laying charges and proceeding through the legal system.

With the rise of social contract theory and constitutional monarchies from the late seventeenth century onward, the sovereign's right to put to death all enemies of the state became subject to further limitations, eventually encompassing the constitutional rights of the accused. But Foucault's brief remarks do not discuss the rise of legal protections for those accused of posing risks to the state. Foucault instead focuses on the question of shifts in the rationale underpinning the state's authority over the life of citizens. In particular, he draws a very sharp contrast between the ancient sovereign right to kill traitors and enemies on the one hand and, on the other hand, the modern state's developing interest in promoting or maximizing life in the aggregate – the life of the nation and the health of the population.

The ancient juridical power to put to death, to execute or otherwise punish traitors and dissenters proceeds, Foucault argues, by 'deduction' or 'subtraction' (Foucault 1980: 136). Those who challenge the sovereign directly or indirectly are regarded as threatening the monopoly of the sovereign over political power, in this type of 'sovereign' political system. Therefore, the power and the freedom and even the life of these dissident or rebellious subjects, can be taken away. The sovereign can execute them or seize their goods, or otherwise take coercive measures to restore his or her monopoly of political power. Sovereignty is upheld by ensuring that nobody diminishes or steals any of the sovereign's power. Importantly, old-fashioned sovereigns do not have sophisticated tools to encourage or incentivize desirable behaviours; they have to rely mainly on coercion. In contrast, modern states (of all stripes – communist as well as liberal) have developed forms of political power that are not deductive, that is, are not based on the zero-sum game of sovereignty.

In the previous chapter we saw how 'discipline' works as an umbrella term, in Foucault's work, for a number of different projects to shape human souls and bodies that do not use the 'deductive' logic of top-down coercion, but rather work in more subtle and productive ways to shape conduct and create disciplined individuals. Discipline is the best-known but by no means the only form of 'positive' (that is, non-deductive) power Foucault documents; as mentioned in the introduction, at different times he discussed 'pastoral' power, governmentality or security, and – the topic of this chapter – biopolitics.

Biopolitics is said to be connected to the rise of market-based, capitalist societies and the accompanying science of political economy. The rise of capitalism and liberal political economy went hand in hand with the emergence of 'population' – population being in Foucault's usage a new entity, one that is visible only at the aggregate level, an entity that is more than (and different from) the sum of the subjects of the sovereign. Modern states take measures that affect populations – that, for example, lower the population's risks or increase the population's health. These are qualitatively distinct from the old juridical measures that act coercively on individuals; but, importantly, they are also distinct from the moralizing and psychologizing effects of discipline. Modern states might undertake measures to increase the population by providing free schooling and/or child tax benefits; or they might instead choose to decrease their population over time, as was the case with China's one-child policy. Such measures of course have to be effected through individuals; and to that extent they may well be accompanied by disciplinary measures aimed, for example, at instilling in parents a sense of the duty to limit births or the duty to vaccinate their children. But even if biopolitical measures have to be taken up and implemented by individuals, their target is not the individual. Their target is either the whole population or certain subpopulations. And their aim is not so much to preserve sovereignty (the rationale of the older 'right to put to death') as to improve, modify, or merely monitor features of 'the population'.

Over time, Foucault's story goes, states began to imagine and govern their citizens not as individual subjects whose loyalty is monitored and governed, but rather as data points serving to constitute populations.[2] Put differently, a state's population comes to be seen not as the sum of atomistic individuals whose private lives are of no particular interest to the sovereign (as long as there is no dissidence) but rather as an aggregate entity with its own features: birth and mortality rates; morbidity rates for various conditions; suicide rates; average level of education; incidence of alcoholism or obesity or diabetes, etc. These features only came to light as it became possible to measure aggregate data with the new tools provided by probability techniques (which had originally been used mainly for gambling purposes but were taken up by early life insurance providers, who had a direct financial interest in accurate calculations of average life expectancies amongst different groups). From mercantilism's focus on the aggregate wealth of the nation to nineteenth-century inventions such as public health inspections, municipal sewers, clean drinking water, and safety measures in factories and mines, over time state power became less concerned with preserving sovereignty and more concerned with the biopolitics of populations.

Deductive or negative power, coercive sovereign power, of course remains a possibility for the state into our own day (as we see in national security mechanisms that take away civil liberties). The potential dissidence of individual subjects of the sovereign is still under scrutiny, especially in the context of anti-terrorist campaigns. But Foucault argues that such coercive uses of power which take away from individual freedom are not the ones that ultimately build modern states. What makes modern states both modern and stable, making them appear not only as legitimate but downright benevolent in the eyes of the people, are the large variety of 'biopolitical' measures that simultaneously increase the power of the state and the health, wealth, and/or well-being of the people, now conceived as a particular aggregate entity – namely population.

In other writings and lectures, on the rise of public health and the origins of urban regulation, Foucault wrote at length about such developments as public health medicine, compulsory vaccinations, and municipal water and sewerage. The novelty of his analyses in these lectures and writings and in the book under discussion was that Foucault saw 'power' at work where others only saw improvement or progress.

A crucial part of Foucault's argument is that this biopolitical power over the collective social-biological life of the nation is two-faced. Many measures (for example, those reducing infant and maternal mortality or reducing the risk of disease transmission) happen to be good for individuals as well as for the state; and, if implemented on a national basis, they improve everyone's wellbeing and help minimize some of the inequality effects of capitalism. But even the most welfare-state oriented form of biopolitical power still has, as its underside and permanent supplement, the power to abandon and even kill certain groups – the power to 'let die' anyone who becomes a threat not so much to the state's legal sovereignty but to the health and wellbeing of the population, the nation, or the race.

The biopolitical threats to the state that different regimes have identified over the years have little to do with the traditional risks to sovereignty (treason, dissidence, political protest). The targets are instead groups, seen as subpopulations rather than as politically organized groups – groups that are seen, for one reason or another, as threatening the collective biopolitical life of the nation and/or the state.

The sterilization and institutionalization of the 'feeble-minded' (that is, low IQ individuals, especially women of child-bearing age) – a programme that was implemented with the full support of law in parts of the US and Canada in the 1910s and 1920s – is an excellent example of such a 'negative' use of biopolitical power. It was the campaign against the 'feeble-minded' that paved the way for later eugenic campaigns. 'Eugenics', or the science of manipulating human reproduction, reached its peak in Nazi claims that many groups – from the mentally handicapped to Slavic peoples to homosexuals to Jews – posed an existential danger to the true German nation. Large-scale murder is committed not for the sake of upholding political sovereignty or defeating a traditional enemy nation, but for the sake of preserving the life of the nation (the true nation). But eugenics can also encompass campaigns to encourage 'the fit' to have more children.

Another useful example of biopolitics at work would be the 'tainted blood' scandals of the late 1980s. In the early days of the AIDS crisis, there was a major moral panic in which haemophiliacs needing regular blood transfusions were presented as the 'innocent' victims, with gay male blood donors who were HIV+ but did not know it (because there was no test or, earlier, because the HIV virus had not yet been identified) constructed as the biopolitical threat to the nation, and especially to vulnerable haemophiliacs. (Haemophiliacs throughout this moral panic were socially constructed as uniformly heterosexual.) Gay men's own health crisis, in the early years, received very little public sympathy; as in other biopolitical moral panics, many people thought that if gay men were falling ill and dying, it was only their own risky behaviour that was to blame. The issue of HIV transmission through blood donations could have been handled in an even-handed and pragmatic manner; but, in keeping with the 'feeble-minded' panic of decades earlier, there was a split made between the 'innocent' and vulnerable nation on the one hand, and a stigmatized, 'risky', threatening subpopulation on the other.

In Canada and Australia, scholars and activists are also using Foucault's notion of biopolitics to describe and theorize historic state policies towards indigenous peoples that were not genocidal in the strong, overtly violent sense, but which involved depriving whole peoples of their land, economic opportunities and, just as importantly, their languages and cultures – which in the end amounts to killing off nations even if many individuals do survive, physically. For example, in Canada today there are heated arguments about whether its history of Native Indian residential schools is best described as 'cultural genocide' (as is generally accepted) or whether the whole array of policies carried out by successive governments to this day constitutes a real, biopolitical genocide – albeit one that developed slowly over time and did not completely succeed. The fact that governments have failed to provide clean drinking water to many northern indigenous communities, sometimes for decades, is a fact that would support such a biopolitical analysis of the Canadian state.

The brilliance and originality of Foucault's analysis here is that mainstream discussions present issues such as the Nazi murder of the mentally and physically handicapped (which laid the basis for the better-known Holocaust of Europe's Jews) or the lack of official concern about clean water in indigenous communities as monumental human rights violations, as blots on the state's claim to be a rule of law state, 'bad' exercises of sovereign juridical power. But Foucault turns completely away from such legal framings. Whether forcibly removing aboriginal children from communities to place them in white-run boarding schools is or is not a crime under international law is, for Foucault, not a useful question; his analysis asks instead: What kind of power is being exercised, exactly, and with what techniques?

Related to the turn away from legal framings and rights talk, an important feature of Foucault's analysis – elaborated at a time, in the late 1970s, when the Cold War was still the overriding global political structure – is that the notion of biopolitics erased or put to one side the then hugely important line supposedly separating liberal states from communist states. More legalistic analyses would read something like the US Supreme Court's endorsement of compulsory sterilization of 'feeble-minded' women in the early twentieth century as a misuse of juridical power, as a betrayal of liberal principles. Along these same rights-oriented lines, liberal-minded people spoke up in the 1980s to denounce and mitigate the stigmatization of gay men in the early days of HIV. But such liberal denunciations of 'human rights abuses' assume that equality and respect are the norm, and that prejudiced attacks on subpopulations thought to be posing a biological or quasi-biological danger to the nation can be ended by means of human rights campaigns. In other words, from a liberal point of view, the darker side of biopolitics can be addressed and overcome through legal rights campaigns and educational means. By contrast, Foucault shows that, far from being abnormal, the all too frequent twentieth-century campaigns to either 'cure' or expel from the body politic or consign to a slow death whole subpopulations are not excesses of prejudice and irrationality. Rather, they are inextricably and systematically connected to the most positive features of modern states (liberal as well as communist), such as the universal provision of health care and social services.

Biopolitics, then, is the name Foucault invents for the specifically modern capacity of modern states to actively promote the life and wellbeing of the population (or the people who count as the population, the nation) while simultaneously retaining the option of treating certain populations (no longer considered as sets of individual citizens) as biomedical dangers to the nation's survival. Whether benignly providing for everyone equally or separating the population into groups, biopolitics works in the same way. From ethnic cleansing, designed to 'purify' certain territories by geographically separating ethnic and/or religious groups, to American state laws banning inter-racial marriage, to the provision of clean drinking water and universal health insurance, biopolitical power is exercised somewhat outside of the whole mechanism of constitutional rights and the rule of law.

To repeat, one and the same type of power – and the same medical, biological, statistical, sociological and moral knowledges of populations and their aggregate health – underpins both the most progressive developments in modern state mechanisms and the most horrifying forms of exclusion. The subpopulations that have at various times been thought of as threats to the nation itself may or may not be citizens, formally. But whether or not they count as citizens for political and legal purposes does not matter very much for biopolitical purposes. Even if they are citizens with legal rights, the imperative to save the health of the nation takes precedence over legal rights – just as it does in compulsory vaccination laws, laws that constitute an excellent example of biopolitics since it is readily apparent that their purpose is to protect the population, and that the protection of the population overrides individual choice.

Foucault's analysis does more than show that the biopolitics of suspicion and division is the other side of the coin whose more benevolent side gave us public health and hygiene as well as social insurance and state health insurance. For Foucault, the two 'sides' of biopolitics do not merely exist side by side – they are actually intertwined. Why? Because eliminating subpopulations regarded as a biopolitical threat can be justified as a positive, quasi-public health measure. For example, the Nazi programme to enslave, displace or simply massacre Slavic peoples was presented as a means toward the desirable, biopolitical end of addressing Germany's overcrowding by gaining more *Lebensraum* – literally, 'room to live'. *Lebensraum*, a noted Nazi slogan, is one of the most clearly biopolitical terms of the twentieth century. Portraying the nation (the Aryan nation, in this case) as in need of large-scale territorial remedies for overcrowding and disease helped enlist the support of middle-of-the-road German people who might not have responded very positively to outright, overt racist claims.

The horror at the centre of modern biopolitics is that massacres – which used to be justified, say, during the time of the Crusades, as what the winning side does when conquering enemy strongholds – may now appear as necessary quasi-public health measures.

> It is as managers of life and survival, of bodies and the race, that so many regimes have been able to wage so many wars, causing so many men to be killed … The atomic situation is now at the end point of this process: the power to expose a whole population to death is the underside of a power to guarantee an individual's continued existence.
>
> (Foucault 1980: 137)

And indeed, during the worst of the Cold War, accumulating vast stockpiles of nuclear weapons was always justified, both in the Soviet camp and among Western powers, as merely defensive, as a measure taken to protect the relevant population from attack.

As mentioned earlier, in the biopolitical frame individuals do not exist on their own (as they do in Hobbes' state of nature, or as they are portrayed in human rights legislation). Individuals are but data points forming a population, with populations becoming visible only through compilations of numbers; and the survival of that modern aggregate entity, population, justifies any measure. The 'juridical existence of sovereignty' is no longer at the centre of either war or punishment: 'at stake is the biological existence of a population.' Foucault then ends the succinct paragraph about genocide and nuclear stockpiling with a sentence that has been repeatedly cited, but which bears re-reading:

> If genocide is indeed the dream of modern powers, this is not because of a recent return of the ancient right to kill; it is because power situated and exercised at the level of life, the species, the race, and the large-scale phenomenon of population.
>
> (Foucault 1980: 137)

'Race' and biopolitics

Neither Foucault's writings and lectures on public health and the history of medicine nor the short section of *The History of Sexuality* that we have been explaining give a systematic explanation of the apparent contradiction between the kind of biopolitical projects that seek to improve all of the nation's population and the biopolitical projects that divide the state's population into quasi-biological groups, seeking then to improve the wellbeing of the 'true' nation by either eliminating, displacing or merely neglecting (and 'letting die') the disfavoured populations.

However, the 1976 lectures at the Collège de France contain an analysis of this important issue (Foucault 2003). In this set of lectures, published only many years after his death, Foucault spends a great deal of time discussing medieval and early modern discourses of honour, blood and nation, discourses produced by aristocrats writing chronicles of the glories of their 'blood', their lineage or their clan. In Britain, stories about the glories of Richard the Lion Heart, Agincourt and so on, which feature the English as a race or nation rather than as citizens within the British state, would be examples of this type of narrative – one that re-emerged centuries later, in the nineteenth century, with the romanticized picture of Saxons during the Norman conquest in Walter Scott's novel *Ivanhoe* (1911) being a good example.

Such non-scholarly, passionate, vivid writings, Foucault argues, were displaced and replaced by the sovereign-centred philosophical discourses of state sovereignty that people like Jean Bodin in France or Hobbes and Locke in England produced.

In the *Society Must be Defended* lectures, Foucault tends to write as if the rational legalistic discourse of sovereignty completely replaced the older, heroic mode of narrating the nation. I would argue, however, that while the older 'race wars' discourse of lineage, blood and honour has been largely eliminated from high culture, from formal law and from the academy, it persists in popular culture. An example of heroic discourse about race in this sense would be the French tales that still circulate today about the brave Gauls who fought against the Roman invasion. These stories have been recycled in romanticized form every century or two, including, in our own day, in the popular Asterix children's book series. In Britain, certain expressions of English, Scottish and Welsh nationalism also draw in more or less explicit ways on this legacy of what Foucault calls 'race struggles.'

Lineages, clans and other kin-based peoples who did not necessarily have a territory or an independent state but had a cohesive identity – based in large part on heroic battles that forged a specific cultural heritage (typically celebrated through epic poems, songs, rituals, flags and crests) – are presented in the 'race' narratives as always opposed to each other, as related through competition if not through outright more or less permanent war. An example that Foucault does not give but which fits very well is the centuries-long war waged in Spain by Christians against the Muslim rulers. To this day, Spanish popular speech counterposes 'Moors' to 'Christians' (for instance, a common playground game where children divide into two teams is called 'Moors and Christians'). The two peoples appear, in this ancient paradigm, as antagonistic cultures inherently opposed to one another by virtue of their lineage and affiliation – a form of conflict that is quite different from that visible among contemporary territorial states whose geopolitical interests may be at odds.

In the 'race wars' paradigm, then – which encourages romantic and non-territorial forms of identification and belonging – Foucault says eliminating the enemy is always justified. And indeed, in the centuries before the rise of modern states and modern political citizenship, the winners of a battle against enemy 'races' would rape the enemy's women and pillage their towns; that was simply the victors' due. But the leaders of each people, clan or lineage had no reason to turn on any subset of their own people (as modern biopolitical programmes do). Indeed, the feudal paradigm of kin and lineage has little or no need to differentiate either the enemy or its own people. Apart from a few celebrated warriors, each 'people' or race in this sense appears as an undifferentiated mass.

One familiar place where one can see this type of proto-political belonging is in Shakespeare's tragedies. Here, a lord may shift his loyalty from one pretender to the throne to another; but once Lord so-and-so makes his move, his retainers and relatives automatically follow, and appear as an undifferentiated mass, like a patriarchal extended family. In *Macbeth* and other stories, sovereignty is contested and fragile, but the clans or lineages reliably act with a unified purpose.

If the mode of belonging differs markedly between one paradigm and the other (heroic 'race' or lineage belonging versus modern sovereign state belonging), so too do the modes of dealing with dissent and resistance. Once state law emerges as a key technique for governing people (with royal or state law being justified through theories of sovereignty), law can be used to eliminate enemies as well as to ensure order and internal peace. But, unlike in the case of Crusade-style massacres of traditional enemies – which were not seen as requiring any particular justification or any inquiry as to who had done what – law has to name specific individuals and make claims about their actions in order to eliminate them. From the witch trials of early modern Europe and the colony of Massachusetts to the show trials of Stalin's Soviet Union, any proceeding initiated by a sovereign state, however unfair, had to build a case against an individual and prove that individual's disloyalty or crime. Laying waste to an enemy city is no longer seen as appropriate (in peacetime at any rate). And punishments of disloyal individuals, including executions, are carried out by the sovereign's representatives, in the name of the sovereign.

The sovereign may eventually become 'the people' with the rise of democracy; but the logic of state law remains the same. Today, criminal prosecutions in the US are styled 'The people of the state of X against Mr. Y', but they do not differ significantly from prosecutions in Britain or Canada, where, formally, it is the monarch that prosecutes.

But while criminal prosecutions, which necessarily target individuals, still invoke the name of the sovereign today (whether 'the people' of a US state or the Queen), forms of power exercised in other spheres do not necessarily proceed through legal actions undertaken in the name of the sovereign. With the rise of contemporary biopolitical rationales of government, sovereigns are not limited to prosecuting individuals in the name of the sovereign. Rather, enemies, internal or external, can be targeted in the name of 'society' by reference to 'the survival of the nation'. Accordingly, those killed under the new biopolitical frame do not have to be identified and prosecuted with specific evidence of wrongdoing or dissidence. Massacres persist and might even flourish and increase, as we have seen in many instances (e.g. the wars in the former Yugoslavia in the 1990s); but massacres that take place in biopolitically oriented regimes and are justified biopolitically are presented as cleansing the nation, rather than eliminating named disloyal individuals.

The key question is then: how is it that a particular modern state, instead of using biopolitical measures strictly to increase the health and wellbeing of its whole population, sometimes uses biopolitical framings to divide the population and identify quasi-biological threats to that nation, a way of dividing people that leaves no recourse to the individuals who might end up being massacred, expelled or deprived of the means of existence? How could the Nazi state, for example, turn from its pioneering public health research into cigarette smoking as a cause of needless death for the population as a whole to its eugenics programme for eliminating whole groups, including all Jews, regardless of political views, intelligence, education or health?

In the 1976 lectures, Foucault suggests that it is 'racism, nothing but racism' that links the otherwise incompatible dimensions of modern biopolitical state power:

> In the biopower system … killing or the imperative to kills is acceptable only if it results not in a victory over political

> adversaries, but in the elimination of the biological threat to and the improvement of the species or race ... *Once the state functions in the biopower mode, racism alone can justify the murderous function of the state.*
>
> (Foucault 2003: 256, emphasis added)

After this lecture, Foucault was asked whether he would like to stress the continuities or the discontinuities between the medieval 'race wars' and the racism of the twentieth century. This is an excellent question, since today's examples of ethnic cleansing and ethnically or religiously justified massacres seem to have strong connections with the older, feudal-era paradigm of blood belonging and lineage. His response, which is very important to appreciate how we might today use the term 'biopolitics' for concrete analyses, was that he prefers to underline the discontinuities between these two meanings of 'race' – no doubt in order to highlight the inglorious role that modern scientific knowledges of human difference have played in justifying measures from the sterilization of low-IQ people to genocide. 'Racism', Foucault says, is a word best preserved for modern, 'biologized' forms of power-knowledge. Modern, biologized racism is thus best distinguished from the pre-biological discourses of honour, blood and race in the sense of lineage that are of far older vintage and have less purchase and less credibility today, even though there are some clear affinities and historic links between these two usages of the term 'race'.

A contemporary example that supports Foucault's preference for historically specifying the meaning of racism and locating it in the context of the rise, in modern Europe, of populations and biopower – rather than seeing racism as a universal tendency of humanity – is the marked shift in the meaning of the term 'race' that has taken place in Canadian discussions about the nation-state since the mid-1970s to mid-1980s. In the 1960s it was still very common to talk about Canada as built by 'two founding races' – and the two races, everyone understood, were the English and the French. This quite ancient meaning of 'race' (meaning something in between a culture and a large extended family) quickly fell into disuse, however, with the renaissance of indigenous politics in the 1980s and after. It would be difficult if not impossible to find any politician in Canada today taking up the language of 'races' when discussing Francophone/Anglophone political struggles. 'Race' now means either the distinction between aboriginal peoples and non-aboriginal peoples or, in other contexts, the distinctions between Asian, white or black people, etc. that are also politically visible in other countries. English Canadians and French Canadians are no longer considered separate races.

The Canadian example suggests that thinking about racism (but not 'race') as a specifically modern phenomenon that is more or less dependent on scientific knowledges may be more useful than seeing it as part of a universal human tendency to be suspicious of others who are somehow now like oneself. In line with this, one current context within which Foucault's ideas about 'biopolitics' has direct resonance is the 'Black Lives Matter' movement, which is certainly concerned with the legal rights of individuals (the right to be treated with respect by police, most immediately), but is also calling attention to 'biopolitical' features of contemporary Western societies.

Those who protest police racial profiling under the 'Black Lives Matter' banner are not merely making a political-legal point about the deprivation of constitutional rights. Movement leaders often discuss the high mortality rates in communities of African descent in the US, and argue that such mortality rates are closely related to the contempt for human life shown by many police officers, but must be addressed through measures that are quite different from those that promote individual rights and face-to-face civility. The civil rights movement of the 1950s and 1960s took a legal-constitutional approach to racial difference and emphasized individual rights, in keeping with contemporary theories of law, state power and sovereignty. By contrast, today – in the US as in other countries with significant black urban populations suffering from discrimination, unemployment and housing segregation – many leaders are taking what one could call a 'biopolitical' approach. Differential mortality and morbidity rates have now become highly politicized. 'Black Lives Matter', arguably, is a slogan that does a great deal more than simply critique police racism and police killings. Foucault might have said that 'Black Lives Matter' is a campaign designed to highlight the ways in which, even after legal equality has been achieved, biopolitical power continues to be exercised, often in impersonal ways, to differentiate populations. Biopolitics, therefore, is a term that can shed light on aspects of governance and politics today that do not concern the legal rights of individuals, but rather the fate of populations.

Notes

1 The 1978–79 series of lectures at the Collège de France, given a couple of years after the original French publication of the first volume of the history of sexuality, was entitled *The Birth of Biopolitics* (2008). However, the main focus on these lectures is the emergence of liberal political economy and specifically the birth of neoliberal economics in the 1950s and onward. The title (which as was the case for all lecture series at the Collège de France, was provided by Foucault far in advance of actually giving the lectures) is not a great guide to the contents.

2 In the interests of fairness it should be said that Foucault's analysis of the rise of 'population' was not completely unique or idiosyncratic. A number of social historians and historians of science were developing similar analyses during the 1970s and 1980s; Ian Hacking is perhaps the most important name amongst them. Hacking's influential work on the history of statistics and probability is in sympathy with Foucault's project but was elaborated independently. See Hacking (1975 and 1990).

Bibliography

Foucault, Michel. 1980. *The History of Sexuality, Vol. I: An Introduction*. New York: Vintage.

Foucault, Michel. 2003. *Society Must Be Defended: Lectures at the Collège de France, 1975–76*. Edited by Mauro Bertani and Allesandro Fontana. Translated by David Macey. New York: Picador.

Foucault, Michel. 2008. *The Birth of Biopolitics: Lectures at the Collège de France, 1978–1979*. Edited by Michel Senellart. Translated by Graham Burchell. New York: Picador.

Hacking, Ian. 1975. *The Emergence of Probability*. Cambridge: Cambridge University Press.

Hacking, Ian. 1990. *The Taming of Chance*. Cambridge: Cambridge University Press.

Scott, Walter. 1911. *Ivanhoe*. Paris: Nelson.

Chapter 4

Governmentality, security, police

This chapter will explain the much-debated and much-used but rather fuzzy term 'governmentality'. Despite the fact that Foucault never gave a clear and stable definition for the invented word and scholars developing his work continue to debate its precise meaning, with no resolution in sight, the word governmentality has launched a thousand ships in various scholarly and public-intellectual environments, including amongst criminological and legal researchers and in areas such as health studies, sexuality studies, social work and sociology. This chapter will explain the term; the next chapter will give some examples of how governmentality has been used within criminological and sociolegal research. (It may perhaps be useful for some readers to read the next chapter first so as to get a sense of why people who are not theorists might want to spend time poring over Foucault's own unfinished and somewhat inconsistent musings on governmentality – and/or my own attempt at explaining the uses of the term.)

But if the purpose of this chapter is to attempt to give a sense of what Foucault intended by inventing and using the term governmentality, why does the title of the chapter feature a set of three terms? Answering this question will begin to address both Foucault's unique methodology (as explained in the introductory chapter) and his reasons for choosing the term governmentality to describe certain shifts in modern governance.

The term governmentality – which, it must be emphasized, Foucault only used in lectures, not in the books published during his lifetime – cannot be understood in isolation. Now, as already mentioned in previous chapters, Foucault avoided giving static definitions of key terms, for theoretical reasons. Instead, he illustrated what his main conceptual terms meant by means of contrasts, sometimes dyadic contrasts (as in sovereignty versus discipline) and sometimes in groups of three terms. In relation to governmentality, numerous scholarly accounts explain governmentality and even provide a definition by contrasting it to both 'sovereignty' and 'discipline' (a useful and influential secondary source along these lines is Mitchell Dean's 1999 book *Governmentality*).

Books and articles along the lines of Dean's helpful overview can be very useful to those who are for the first time trying to grapple with Foucault's ideas. Indeed, in my own teaching practice I have generally used the by now established tripartite scheme also used by Dean: I explain what governmentality is and does by contrasting it first with sovereignty and then with discipline. I tell students that while sovereignty is a top-down form of power that comes down on people only at certain times, and which relies on public punishments in the domestic realm and on war in external relations, disciplinary regimes exercise a more continuous and fluid power by means of sophisticated knowledge-based techniques such as examination, observation and normalization. In turn, governmentality is a term used to describe those even more sophisticated and modern exercises of power that involve turning authority's gaze away from individual bodies and souls (the main targets of discipline) and fixing it instead on populations and their characteristics, rendered visible and calculable in aggregate data. Statistics and probability are thus key knowledge forms for governmentality, whereas biomedical and moral-social knowledges of deviance and normality are the bread and butter of disciplinary projects. As discussed in the previous chapter, sovereign power has a limited interest in knowing its subjects, being interested mainly in whether the subjects of the sovereign are loyal or disloyal. By contrast, both discipline and governmentality depend in fundamental ways on gaining knowledge of the individuals and populations being governed; and, to that extent, discipline and governmentality cannot always be sharply separated from one another – the neat contrast drawn by

Foucault between sovereign punishment and expert-led discipline does not have a parallel in comparisons of discipline and governmentality.

Governmentality, in my view, is best described as an umbrella term covering an indeterminate range of exercises of knowledge and power – it is not a clearly defined concept with a fixed content or meaning. It is a term Foucault uses to highlight similarities linking a variety of governing practices that do not directly bear down on individuals, or even on specific groups, but rather work impersonally through the collection of data and the calculation of the efficient ways of managing collective risks. Governmentality is not the same as liberal economics, since it covers spheres far from the economic; but 'governmental' projects often use quasi-economic logics. They generally seek to incentivize rather than punish, and to guide rather than to coerce, usually appealing to individuals' own desire for freedom of choice along the way. 'Here are the numbers on cigarette smoking and cancer: you now choose what's good for you' would be a typical governmentality way of trying to get people to stop smoking, for example. Such an approach is clearly different from a sovereign command to prohibit the sale of cigarettes altogether, and also from the disciplinary work of family doctors and nurses who try to coax their patients, one at a time, into quitting.

So far so good; the tripartite scheme of sovereignty, discipline and governmentality clearly does provide guidance and a language for analyses of how we are governed and how we govern ourselves and others. However, reflecting on my experience of using a handy three-column chart to explain Foucault's analysis of power and knowledge to students (Table 4.1), it now seems to me that such stark contrasts between governmentality, sovereignty and discipline, which have been endlessly repeated and simplified in numerous articles and books as well as in teaching materials, may fail to do justice to Foucault's methodological choices. The three-column chart that I have used for years, shown here, is very useful heuristically and has been positively received by numerous cohorts of students. But it has to be admitted that the chart bears an all-too comfortable resemblance to epochal schemes popular in classical sociology, such as Marx's

Table 4.1 Foucault's analytical tools for the study of governing practices

Sovereignty	*Discipline*	*Governmentality*
Juridical yes-or-no rules as typical format of power	Norms (statistical or clinical) as key format of power	Risk calculations as key format of power
Aim: preserving sovereign authority	Aim: creating normalized individuals	Aim: securing territories and populations; constituting responsible individuals
Key personnel: state officials	Key personnel: experts (especially psych and medical)	Expertise still key, but working through individuals and their choices
Punishment as key control technique, domestically: warfare as key technique for external relations	Normalization of bodies through disciplinary techniques – over time, formation of modern 'self'	Governing through freedom: incentives, teaching people to make the 'right' choices
Typical technique: spectacles (the many watching the one)	Surveillance: the one watching the many Hierarchical observation Examination	Risk calculations Risk management
The governed: loyal subjects	The governed: disciplined individuals	Autonomous, self-directed, entrepreneurial citizens and consumers – and healthy and prosperous populations

theory of history, which has feudalism replaced by capitalism and socialism eventually displacing capitalism.

Now, while Foucault does indeed claim that sovereignty is much older and governmentality is of more recent vintage – with discipline being at its height in the era from the mid-nineteenth to the mid-twentieth century – if the chart presented here is interpreted as if it were an account of 'eras' or epochs that rise and fall smoothly over time that would be misleading. Epochal schemes simply do not do justice to the flexibility and tentativeness and historical specificity of Foucault's thought. Apart from misrepresenting Foucault's underlying methodological aims, such epochal schemes, if used in cookie-cutter manner to 'explain' this or that phenomenon, may also have the negative effect of closing down paths for research instead of opening them. It is too easy to simply reify Foucault's terms and proceed to collect 'instances' of discipline or sovereignty or governmentality. That type of classificatory work – often described, to my dismay, as 'applying theory' – goes completely against the grain of the creative, open-ended and site-specific logic of Foucault's own work.

If Foucault never gave a clear, stable, textbook-like definition of governmentality, and thus refused to play the social science game of producing ideas and conceptual terms that function as static theories that students and empirical researchers can simply plunk down and 'apply', it was for a very good, theoretically based reason. The reason why I argue that Foucault's terminology ought not to be used to play the conventional social science game of definitions and 'examples' is that terms like governmentality must be understood not as clearly defined concepts but rather as provisional and context-specific generalizations. Foucault's goal was never to stuff historical and contemporary instances of power/knowledge into the 'correct' categories; it was always to shed light on actually existing situations, emphasizing their contingency, precariousness and open-endedness. Some of his work (especially in *Discipline and Punish*) shows the lingering effects of the structuralist mindset of the 1960s and 1970s, and to that extent sounds somewhat deterministic; but in Foucault's most creative moments, he insists that undertaking genealogies of modern governing practices is a task designed to underline the fact that things could have turned out otherwise. Power relations, even when very asymmetrical, and even when they have been 'naturalized' so that they look inevitable, are never fixed or omnipotent. Most classic sociology or political science frameworks read history looking only for causes of the present, which has the effect of making the present seem nearly inevitable. The precariousness of power is perhaps not a theme that most readers would see in Foucault's work; but, in my reading, Foucault's work breaks with the determinism that afflicted both Marxist and liberal theories of power current in his lifetime, and emphasizes the instability of power.

Foucault's constant insistence that power is everywhere is not meant to deny asymmetries; but it is meant to emphasize that there is no binary opposition between those who govern and those who are governed. In Foucault's framework, subordinate or subaltern groups can and do exercise some forms of power, in relation to their own members or to other groups as well as in relation to the powers that be. This view made Foucault somewhat unpopular in certain activist circles; for example, in relation to gay rights, Foucault suggested that the gay movement itself might be promoting a certain view of authentic personal sexual identity that exercised a certain disciplinary and governmental force over its own members. The naïve notion that some people or groups are exercising pure 'resistance' when they engage in political action was one that was very popular in the 1970s and beyond, but that Foucault's understanding of power showed to be deficient.

Returning to the question of the status of conceptual terms including governmentality, Foucault's refusal to play the social science game of 'applying' theory does not mean that generalizations are impossible and that we are stuck with an infinite set of wholly particular descriptions. The point is that it is actual social, economic, moral, political and legal relations that are real, with notions like sovereignty and governmentality having a certain utility as tools that can identify and name affinities and similarities between different governing projects, but without ever becoming ends in themselves – as is the case with most 'concepts' produced by conventional social science, which come to seem more real than the reality they supposedly represent and describe.

Thus, here, while I will make some use of the contrasts between governmentality on the one hand and discipline and sovereignty on the other, I will proceed mainly by highlighting the *overlaps* between governmentality and two other terms used by Foucault to understand modern state power: 'security' and 'police'.

It must be said right away that the discussion of police in this chapter will not be wholly faithful to what Foucault says about police in much of his work on the subject; but I feel it better reflects the reality of governance today, especially in nation-states (including virtually all common law jurisdictions) with relatively strong traditions of local authority jurisdiction and judicial deference towards those local authorities. In Foucault's own account, at least the detailed account in the 1977–78 lectures at the Collège de France (Foucault 2007), *governmentality* is presented largely as a rejection of the logic of *police* – police here meaning not police forces but rather the emerging systems of administrative and regulatory measures to create order, especially in the urban context, that flourished in the seventeenth and eighteenth centuries. 'Police' regulations comprise the complex web of detailed, often highly specific regulations that, beginning as local, city-based rules about markets, cleanliness, safety and morals (rules justified as promoting *salus populi*, 'the people's welfare'), became – when taken up by promoters of what was called 'police science' (public administration, essentially) – a key tool of what we call 'the administrative state'. Now, Foucault relied to some extent on the works produced by early economists, who criticized the ways in which traditional police logics (e.g. governments worried about urban revolts imposing a maximum price for bread) stymied not only individual enterprise but also the state's own prosperity. Since these writers (Adam Smith, for example, who acknowledged that police is necessary but classified it as an inferior part of government) elaborated their ideas about economics and about the role of the state by criticizing traditional police regulations, Foucault – whose lectures on governmentality are mainly commentaries on texts such as those produced by Smith – gives the impression that the rise of liberalism in economic and in politics in fact displaces and replaces police. But, as I will go on to argue, a more thorough appreciation of legal history, especially in the English-speaking world (in which police takes a different, much less politically visible form than in highly centralized states like France or Russia) is necessary in order to properly use Foucault's ideas today.

Today, in the common law world and in many parts of the civil law world, alongside the governmentality mechanisms that monitor aggregate data and incentivize certain activities in an impersonal manner there are also highly intrusive police mechanisms of older vintage, mainly designed to micromanage spaces and activities, both public and private, in classic police-regulation style. A classic example would be a rule banning sleeping in city parks. These powers tend to be exercised at the local scale rather than nationally, and so they usually escape the notice of social scientists focusing on how power works at the scale of the nation-state.

I will show throughout this chapter, then, that despite the proliferation and increased sophistication of neoliberal governmental techniques that govern without overt coercion or even without acting on persons directly, the logic of police regulation is by no means diminished, even though its operations are now subject to some legal limits due to the rise of human rights and other state-level legal and political mechanisms. But first we will discuss 'security' in relation to 'governmentality.'

Governmentality and security

Foucault introduced the term governmentality in early 1978 in the course of a series of lectures that had been advertised under the title 'Security, Territory, Population' (2007). The neologism is introduced in the second lecture, but it is only in the fourth that it assumes a central position. There, Foucault told his audience that if he had been able to re-title the lecture series after having worked on them, he would have chosen to replace the word 'security' with the word 'governmentality'.

> Basically, if I had wanted to give the lectures I am giving this year a more exact title, I certainly would not have chosen 'Security, territory, population'. What I would really like to undertake is something that I would call a history of 'governmentality.' By the word 'governmentality' I mean three things. First, by 'governmentality' I understand the ensemble formed by institutions, procedures, analyses and reflections, calculations and tactics that allow the exercise of this very specific … power that has the population as its target, political economy as its major form of knowledge, and apparatuses of security as its essential technical instrument.
>
> (Foucault 2007: 108)

The translator's phrase 'apparatuses of security' may be misleading, and so an explanation is in order. In French, there are two different words for what in English is simply called 'security'. One, *sécurité*, refers to the prevention and management of risks – for example, social security is *sécurité sociale*. The other word is *sûreté*. *Sûreté* is a somewhat Hobbesian term referring to the state's own preservation; thus, the police force of Quebec is called *Sûrete du Québec*. The phrase 'apparatuses of security', which in the French original has *sécurité*, does not refer to police forces and border officials and so on. Instead, it refers to the very broad array of mechanisms that states use to monitor activities and populations and ensure future stability and prosperity. These may include bodies of uniformed officials, perhaps even armed officials; but the emphasis is on proactively managing future risks, with economic risks and risks to the nation's human resources at the centre of concern.

The logic of security in this sense is thus quite distinct from the logic of sovereignty. Denying an immigrant entry to a country for 'security' reasons is an exercise of sovereignty; implementing a policy to attract certain professionals to move to a country, by contrast, is a strategy of security/governmentality that uses incentives to secure the population, and especially the labour force.[1] Maintaining security is difficult for modern states not only because on occasion individual liberty may clash with governmental plans to secure the population or the nation, but also because with the rise of modern economic and social relations a whole new set of entities emerges that need to be secured: public health, electricity supplies, transit systems, airports and air travel, financial markets, etc.

It should now be clear why the term 'governmentality' arose in the context of Foucault's analysis of the history of state projects aiming to secure capitalist economic production and trade. 'Security' in this sense is not state security in the sense of uniformed officers and anti-terrorist units, but rather the preventive management of risks of all sorts, from the economic to the biopolitical. It should also be clear why liberal political economy is given a central role in the rise of governmentality. Liberal political economy provided a new framework, or perhaps more modestly, a model for all manner of governing projects; it was not merely a set of policies for governing strictly economic matters like foreign trade, wage labour and commodity prices. The general trend towards governing *with* markets and with individual desires rather than against them slowly extended to non-economic fields.

For instance, health risks, once thought to be the exclusive domain of omniscient physicians, are now said to be requiring management by patients themselves. Physicians used to tell patients: have this operation, take this medication, etc. The trend towards giving patients risk information about a possible operation or about taking a drug, and letting them decide which course to pursue, is an excellent instance of governmentality. The health care system is acting in a less sovereign, less top-down manner and is instead governing medical procedures *through and with patients' own desire for knowledge and choice*. Of course, health care professionals still exercise a great deal of influence (as they should, since the average patient does not necessarily have the capacity to make a truly informed choice, always a thorny problem for governmental projects that would work through our freedom); but the model of governance is one in which patient choice, instead of appearing as a threat to doctors' power, is maximized, and often recruited in the service of better health care delivery.

Returning to the historical rise of governmentality, elsewhere in the lectures Foucault talks about the rise of governmentality by contrasting it with older genres of political writing designed to help sovereigns maintain their monopoly of power, for example through the doctrine of 'reason of state'. From the late eighteenth century to today, the reason of state idea has been used to justify state secrecy and extraordinary national security measures. By contrast with this top-down, state monopoly of power doctrine, early writers on what they called 'government' and Foucault calls 'governmentality' emphasized the overlaps and affinities between non-political and political power. In the new paradigm, governing one's children or governing one's emotions are partly planned and partly pragmatic activities that are both similar to and can be a model for a new form of political power, one exercised not against people in a top-down manner but rather by guiding and rewarding, providing information and incentivizing. As Foucault put it elsewhere, governmentality 'was understood in the broad sense of techniques and procedures for directing human behaviour. Government of children, government of souls and consciences, government of a household, of a state, of oneself' (Foucault 1997: 82). And those who govern their children or their own souls do it best with the least possible coercion– at their best, they work *with* the entities or people being governed, not against them.

Governmentality can thus encompass a very wide variety of efforts to guide human conduct, preferably by using impersonal means, and in such a way as to align the interests and objectives of the authorities with individuals' desire for knowledge, freedom and choice. Here we can begin to see why political economy is said to be the primary form of knowledge at work in governmental projects. Liberal political economy exhorts governments to interfere with private enterprise as little as possible, and only to foster production and trade. Liberal political economists like Adam Smith railed against absolutist government's tendency to ban exports or ban imports, to set high tariffs and control the prices of basic consumer goods. It is not that government ought to withdraw completely, but rather that government policies ought to be based on data about what is good for 'the economy', and ought to incentivize those activities that will have the most beneficial effects, however those are defined. For Smith and for liberal economists since, free enterprise tends to organize itself, with government activity being seen as necessary (e.g. to issue currency and provide a legal system) but also being regarded with some suspicion, as a potential spanner in the works of a system that has its own logic and its own self-correcting mechanisms. The wise government, in liberal terms, is one that gathers data that will serve to gently guide economic and non-economic activity in the direction of peace and prosperity; it will not take drastic coercive measures.

Finally, while sovereign power only requires knowledge of whether citizens are loyal or not, governmentality uses masses of information about populations – aggregate data – to guide the conduct of individuals and groups in a largely impersonal manner and to guide its own policy work. For that reason, there can be much overlap between biopolitics, as discussed in the previous chapter, and governmentality: both modes of governing are heavily dependent on aggregate data, and both modes are future-oriented. In empirical studies of real-life governing projects one might well find that there is no real dividing line between biopolitics and governmentality. However, treating them as separate notions or terms, analytically, helps to stress that biopolitics has no particular attachment to either liberal ideas in law or free-market economic mechanisms. Totalitarian governments can and do use biopolitical measures in ways that go against the logic of liberal governmentality.

In Foucault's analysis in the 1977–78 lectures at the Collège de France (and elsewhere), governmentality builds on and encourages liberal economic knowledge, but its scope is by no means limited to economic matters. The same governance trends can be found in many projects undertaken by contemporary states. Health care delivery's transformation in recent years under the banner of informed consent and patient empowerment has already been mentioned; in addition, social welfare programmes now often use labour market aggregate data to guide unemployed applicants to particular fields and particular training programmes, or even to persuade them to move to another part of the country, but without ever directly coercing people into moving or into particular professions or trades. That could be described as a 'governmentalization' of labour markets – and the governmentalization of workers themselves.

The government of others and the government of the self

Foucault's long-standing effort to link the government of others to the governance of oneself was based on a belief – which seems to have grown stronger as he aged– that the separation of ethics from economics and politics is a somewhat problematic development. By returning to Greek, Roman and early Christian sources, later in his life, Foucault tried to find inspiration to critique the way in which modern governance (and the modern academy) separates questions of ethics from economic and political decision-making. This effort to shed critical light on the modern world's separation of ethics from politics led Foucault to always underline that it is not just authorities that govern us according to various governmental logics. We too govern ourselves in this governmental fashion. An example would be the way in which many of us keep track of calories consumed at the table or calories burned at the gym – as if our bodies were mini-economies in need of fine-tuning. The calorie-counting exercise, which is never without a moral connotation, shows not only that we can use governmentality logics originally developed in the economic realm to govern non-economic conduct, but also that ethical and moral norms are still very much with us, even amongst those of us who are completely secular and even atheistic.

The most important point here is that, contrary to the Marxist notion of the 'critique of ideology' that was widely accepted in the 1970s, Foucault is *not* saying that the discourse of empowerment, individual choice, autonomy and even freedom that is common in governmentality projects is a lie. The freedom of choice that is promised and in many ways delivered by various governmentality projects, both those we choose and those that are foisted on us, is neither a lie nor an illusion, as Marxist critics would have it. Foucault's work broke sharply with the Marxist idea that freedom under capitalism is just an illusion, and argued that governmentality does actually work through individuals' desire for freedom and autonomy, not against it. In that sense freedom of choice is real. But – and a very important 'but' – exercising that autonomy properly is understood (usually implicitly) as necessarily linked to socially desirable activities and goals. Graduation-card clichés such as 'to thine own self be true', 'live your dreams', etc. do in fact promote personal autonomy, and people who buy graduation cards containing such messages are no doubt sincere in their wishes for the graduate. But Foucault would point out that the same slogans are also used by authorities who have very distinct ideas about what is an appropriate dream or how exactly one should be true to oneself.

Becoming a successful drug dealer would not count as a valid personal 'dream', for example; and any young person who claimed that avoiding both school and work is how they plan to remain true to themselves would soon find that there are limits to being governed through one's freedom.[2] Thus, the freedom of choice inherent in governmentality projects is real enough; but we are indeed governed, including morally governed, through and by our very desire to be autonomous and exercise choice.

How discourses of freedom and autonomy are currently used so as to hide from view the intense moral regulation that still exists in the most governmentally advanced regimes will be taken up in the next chapter, where we will summarize research done by Foucaultian criminologists. For now, however, we will return to Foucault's own work and continue unpacking 'governmentality', now in relation to 'police'.

Governmentality and police

In the course of Foucault's meandering discussion of the history of various forms of power, interpersonal as well as political, in the 1977–78 lectures, Foucault moves slowly into the early modern era. As he does so he focuses his gaze more narrowly on the state, leaving the non-state forms of power analysed in the earlier lectures somewhat to the side. Here is where we find a fascinating if incomplete discussion of 'police' – a term that, as mentioned above, is of much older vintage and covers a great deal more than the work of modern constabularies (Lecture on March 29, 1978, Foucault 2007: 311–32). As it happened, that particular lecture was somewhat delayed because Foucault, as he breathlessly explained, was stuck in one of Paris's notorious traffic jams. This apparently trivial incident could not be more apt. The regulation of all manner of traffic in the service of the smooth circulation of people, goods and wealth was one of the key objects, if not the key object, of the new arts of governance developed in the eighteenth century by French state officials, and by assorted thinkers working in the dukedoms and mini-states in what later became Italy and Germany. Much of this work took place under the banner of 'police science', meaning not the study of police forces (which did not yet exist) but the study of the best means of arranging domestic affairs. And at the legal level, police regulations (ordinances or bylaws, essentially) were developed to create, secure and improve transportation routes. Traffic was thus a key problem and target of police governance, and remains so to this day. The particular means used to ship goods and get around and send communications have of course changed over the centuries; but the basic legal powers used to promote circulation and traffic and communication have remained remarkably constant.

It is crucial to note that in the eighteenth century – that is, well before there were any organized, professional constabularies much less national police forces – the word 'police' had a fairly settled meaning as one of the three key dimensions of state power. The diplomatic-military dimension of state power was routinely distinguished from the 'revenue' function (which included taxation, mainly, but also tariffs and tolls). And both of these were in turn distinguished from 'police', understood as the regulatory and preventive governance of the internal order and tranquillity of the kingdom.

Just as the state is the location, or the scale of government, that suits military, diplomatic and fiscal measures, urban space was (and remains) the site par excellence of police power and police regulations. Cities in Europe had, since medieval times, regulated all manner of things. They set down detailed rules about who could sell what goods where and at what times; where dangerous trades or morally risky businesses could be located; who could manufacture what items according to what standards; where trash and waste should be placed; and how citizens ought to act in case of a plague or other threatening disease. Cities also had the power to demolish buildings that stood in the way of public works or that constituted a threat to the health or welfare of the community, a power that remains strong to this day (although today owners generally have to be compensated). And cities also had – and continue to have – the power to compel citizens to help maintain the public realm and keep up aesthetic standards. A somewhat trivial example that may illustrate this is that, today, citizens who want to place a sign on their own private property require a municipal permit. In many cases, such as on residential streets, such signs are completely banned, with the minor exception of political party signs during elections: that is a small indication of the great power that local authorities have over private property. Similarly, billboards cannot be erected by the simple means of an advertiser signing a contract for rent with the owner of the land in question; billboards require municipal permits and are banned from many locations, for purely aesthetic reasons. Commenting on treatises that attempted to collate the multifarious regulations that made up the field of police, Foucault concludes that 'to police and to urbanize are the same thing' (2007: 344).

As briefly mentioned in relation to Foucault being stuck in a traffic jam, transportation (inside cities and between them) was a crucial arena for the development of what in the US eventually came to be called 'the police power of the state' – that is, the power, usually local, to issue 'police regulations' that arrange economic activities spatially and temporally, and that greatly limit what property owners can do with their property. Harbours, ports, rivers, roads, bridges and markets were objects and targets of police regulations; but all of this infrastructure was also itself produced by exercising the legal powers of police. For example, a toll might be charged to ferry users, with the money collected being later used to build a bridge that would make the ferry unnecessary; and, along the way, police powers could be deployed to expropriate and/or demolish any building that stood in the way of the desired bridge. Most of the transportation infrastructure of Europe and North America, before the twentieth century, was built privately. But the police power was used by local, county and state authorities to assemble the land required for the infrastructure, and to eliminate potential competition for the successful bidders or concessionaires (as is still the case today, when for-profit toll highways or public-private partnerships are created through an array of legislative actions that in many cases detract from other private owners' property rights).

The police power exercised by local (or sometimes state- or county-level) authorities was and remains very great, and very intrusive. However, because police power is exercised more over activities, spaces and economic opportunities than directly over persons, it does not have much political visibility. For example, today cities use their police power to charge drivers rent for parking their vehicles on streets that their taxes have already paid for; but there are no social movements devoted to eliminating parking charges. In any case it would not be possible, legally, to use personal rights arguments to have courts strike down zoning bylaws and ordinances or bylaws setting out parking fees and fines. Courts would say that parking is not a right but a privilege, and that the municipality, not the citizens, owns the streets – a classic 'police' statement.

Similarly, no argument about constitutional rights to freedom of movement would ever prevail against the compulsion exercised by traffic lights and traffic signals. And no doctrine of commercial freedom would suffice, in law, to strike down the myriad regulations governing the sale of alcoholic beverages. In law, but to a large extent also in people's own sense of what is right and wrong, the power of local authorities to take proactive measures to ensure efficient circulation and protect the health and welfare of 'the people' trumps the vast majority of individual rights claims.

If the *content* or object of police governance is generally to ensure that urban space is orderly and the movement of people, goods and vehicles is efficient, police also takes a distinctive *form*. A format that is typical of police regulation is the long list of heterogeneous entities and activities subject to a particular form of regulation. Examples here would be the list of the types of business that require a municipal licence or the list of measurements that defines particular kinds of property for zoning purposes (e.g. height and mass limits for dwellings; distance of house from sidewalk; minimum yard sizes; maximum size of paved parking area).

Foucault points out that Catherine the Great's Russian police regulations manual states that law is composed of general *rules*, whereas police works through detailed *lists* of dos and don'ts. The distinction between laws of general application, justified by grand principles, and local regulations that take the form of somewhat random lists is more politically visible in French law and administration than in common law countries. French governments have long worked with a clear separation of *loi de police* and *loi de justice* (the law of police and the law of justice) – with the former associated with administrative regulation and the latter with criminal justice or civil lawsuits.[3] Constitutional rights are justified and prefaced by general claims ('all men are created equal', for instance) and they are rationally organized in texts that provide grand philosophical foundations as well as specific legal measures. But police regulations, which are often a series of one-at-a-time pragmatic responses to problems, lack such general justifications. Why city A requires barbers to be licensed whereas city B, across the road, only requires pawnbrokers and fireworks sellers and restaurants to be licensed but not barbers is not the kind of question that is likely to have a highly conceptual or even a clearly political answer.

In general, authorities acting under the banner of the police power are always seeking particular solutions to specific, ever-changing problems, often under conditions in which some local political actor simply pushes successfully for one regulation rather than another, for some contingent and often highly local reason unlikely to have been recorded in official history. For example, zoning rules decreeing that a liquor store or a porn shop must be located at least 1,000 feet or 1,000 metres from the nearest other one are typical police regulations in two ways: they combine moral with other risks/harms; and they also use quite arbitrary and unscientific numbers, contrary to the governmentality-biopolitics logic of using aggregate data as evidence to guide policy. My favourite example of police-style non-scientific numbers is the New York City ordinance that forbids dogs from barking for more than a specified number of minutes, the actual number varying according to whether it is day or night – such variation being also typical of police regulation formats.

If urban space was the first and continues to be the main target of the detail-oriented, pragmatic micromanagement project that is the police power, this does not mean the police power is completely impersonal. Traditionally, a key aim of police regulations was to control and limit the movement of 'vagrants' and other disreputable characters (e.g. sex workers, entertainers and itinerant vendors). Today it is no longer legally permissible for local authorities to issue regulations applying only to the poor or only to homeless people; but the myriad regulations that micromanage the activities that can take place in spaces like public squares, public transit, schoolyards and parks are often directed, indirectly or directly, at street people.

Police and capitalism: a contradictory relationship

In the governmentality lectures Foucault explains that police, as a mode of power, is distinct from but closely connected to discipline, governmentality and biopolitics. Police regulations organize space to maximize the circulation of goods, workers and customers, and in addition target both the health risks and the moral risks that are inherent in the urban condition. Therefore, the work of police lays the foundations for capitalist economies, and thus for governmentality, as well as providing the legal underpinnings for the exercise of biopolitical power. And police regulations have disciplinary effects either on everyone or on particular groups (such as the homeless people who may have wanted to sleep in parks).

But if the work of police facilitates capitalism and governmentality, the micromanagement that is inherent in police regulations also acts, simultaneously, as a brake on capitalism. Police regulations, for example, long prevented anyone who was not part of a certain merchant guild from making and selling certain commodities, which certainly put a brake on potential capitalists; police regulations also limited the number and the opening times of municipal marketplaces, and banned any buying and selling in places other than those marketplaces. Police regulations also limited what private real estate owners could do with their properties (which is still the case – it is the police power that prevents homeowners from opening a profitable pub or store in their front room).

Because Foucault uses French, German, Italian and Russian sources – rather than looking at the common law world – he tends to over-emphasize the top-down and even absolutist uses of police powers, and fails to recognize the crucial distinction between different scales of governing, between local authority and state power. Thus, Foucault writes that 'police is the direct governmentality of the sovereign as sovereign'; police is 'the permanent coup d'état' (Foucault 2007: 347). That is somewhat misleading. Because the sovereign (state-level) and specifically absolutist uses of police knowledge and police power are so heavily emphasized in Foucault's account, due to the location or the prejudices of his sources, the liberal revolution that transformed both law and economics is presented as the negation of police, rather than as a revision or modification of police powers and techniques that left police powers at the local level largely untouched while putting limits on what central states could do by way of micromanaging and monitoring citizens.

The governmentalization of the state

Having throughout emphasized that 'governmentality' is not a political theory, and is not a way of governing that is exclusive to the state, Foucault talks about the 'governmentalization' of modern states (Foucault 2007: 355). The reason he uses this somewhat awkward formulation is to emphasize the continuities between different spheres or scales of governing. As mentioned above, governmentality is a term that has been found very useful by scholars who analyse recent trends in health care delivery or in social work and social services, as well as by criminologists; and many governing practices that we choose for ourselves, to govern our food intake or our exercise or our education, can also be usefully said to be 'governmental'. At a time – the late 1970s – when most critical thinkers were obsessed with the idea of 'theorizing the state', Foucault's bold approach de-centred the state and highlighted the ways in which governing practices and governing rationales can and do float and shift from one realm to another, without regard for the supposed boundaries separating the state, civil society and the family.

The discussion of the governmentalization of the modern state includes a comment on how liberal governmentality arose out of a rejection of the logic of police (Foucault 2007: 355). As just mentioned, this is true as far as the intellectual history of governmentality and liberal economic thought is concerned; certainly Adam Smith, as previously mentioned, made much of his view that French police regulations were greatly hindering economic development while not actually securing urban order, and relied on a caricatured view of continental police regulations in order to promote his own ideas about letting the capitalist economy flourish according to its own laws. But the relationship between police and liberal governance (of the economy or of the state itself) was not in fact as antagonistic as portrayed in Foucault's sources.

International police?

A final feature of the discussion of police in the *Security, Territory, Population* lectures is one with great relevance to today's 'war on terror', and also to the global governance of state finances through bodies such as the International Monetary Fund (IMF) and the World Bank. Departing from the conventional eighteenth-century view of police as the domestic ordering of the kingdom, Foucault tells his audience (with very few references, unfortunately) that police methods and police action are not always confined to internal domestic matters. The European equilibrium of states established by the Treaty of Westphalia (1648), Foucault argues, is also a site of and for police. Each of the European states – and Europe is defined as a plurality of states in equilibrium, a diagram of power that is elsewhere contrasted to the unified and expansive logic of empire (Foucault 2007: 294–300) has to treat the internal order and even the economy of other states as integral to its own welfare. 'Equilibrium is only maintained to the extent to which each of the states is capable of increasing its own strength [but] at a rate that does not threaten other states' (ibid.: 322). Therefore, each state, in Europe at any rate, must be assured that other states are minding their own order, their own police. 'The European equilibrium thus functions as a sort of inter-state police or inter-state law. The European equilibrium gives the community of states the right to make sure that police matters are in good order in each of its states' (ibid.).

That some decades after Foucault's death the European banking authorities would draw up regulations for the internal ordering of the Greek economy, as well as imposing certain standards on states seeking to join the European Union (EU), are phenomena that are clearly foreseen in this fascinating passage. In addition, Foucault's remarks on how the 1815 Treaty of Vienna set up the possibility for intervening in other states' internal affairs if the government in question failed to establish a proper form of internal police also foreshadow the doctrine of 'humanitarian intervention' that was used to justify the Iraq war and other contemporary armed interventions. These remarks are in fact far more relevant to today's world situation than they were in the Cold War, two-superpower world of 1978.

Governmentality and liberal governance

It was mentioned above as an important point that Foucault never published any of his work on governmentality during his lifetime. As a result, the lectures that are now available contain one crucial ambiguity. The ambiguity is that sometimes the term 'governmentality' is used in such a way that it is coterminous with liberal political economy, or even liberal governance more generally – but at other times the term is used to refer to any settled pattern of governance, as in a quote used a few paragraphs above about how 'police is the direct governmentality of the sovereign as sovereign'.

Much scholarly ink has been spent – perhaps too much – debating whether the term 'governmentality' should be identified with liberal governance or whether it can be used more neutrally and capaciously, as in 'the governmentality of the early Church' or 'the governmentality of the Chinese Communist Party'. In my view, arguments amongst scholars about whether Foucault 'really' meant to equate governmentality with liberal governance are misleading, to the extent that such arguments assume one can determine a fixed, static meaning for the term 'governmentality'. It is more appropriate and helpful to simply recognize that in the work on governmentality and the genealogy of modern states Foucault's key interest was in developing a non-Marxist but nevertheless critical and left-wing analysis of the rise of liberal mechanisms for governing both economic and non-economic processes. But this does not mean that either Foucault or scholars today are somehow inconsistent or 'wrong' if they use phrases such as 'the governmentality of the Chinese Communist Party' or 'the colonial governmentality of the British Empire in India'. The historical roots of governmentality in what was called simply 'government' allow for such somewhat expansive uses of the term. To avoid confusion, however, it is probably advisable to include the term 'liberal' (or more specifically neoliberal, in relation to certain contemporary projects) along with 'governmentality', if that is one's object of study. Current shifts in how states such as Australia and Canada govern indigenous peoples, for example, can be usefully described as borrowing techniques and discourses from liberal governmentality (e.g. devolving the power and the responsibility to provide education or health to indigenous communities themselves, under the banner of self-determination). But if one finds it useful to differentiate those white settler state practices that seem to produce liberal governmentality from those that produce old-fashioned paternalistic colonial governmentality, and speak about two contradictory governmentalities coexisting in a single space, that could help illuminate the multiple contradictions of contemporary governance – a goal not inconsistent with Foucault's own approach.

Thus, 'governmentality' was a term that Foucault developed to a large extent due to his interest in the genealogy of liberal economic governance and the expansion of this model of governance to other fields of life. Nevertheless there is no law against using the term 'governmentality' in a broader fashion to describe other, not necessarily liberal patterns of governance, patterns that are rarely the product of a systematic plan but are not unique, being commonly found across many locations. In the following chapter we will see examples of what contemporary criminologists and sociolegal scholars have done when using the resources of governmentality to analyse various contemporary mechanisms of governance: some that govern through our freedom of choice and our desire to be autonomous, and some that definitely limit choice in illiberal ways. For Foucault the question would always be: how well are you capturing the complexity of actually existing governance practices? Definitions were always regarded with suspicion by Foucault; in the end, if the tools of governmentality can help us provide a full and accurate picture, that is what matters.

Notes

1 In Britain writers like Jeremy Bentham discussed 'security' in these governmental terms, and indeed Foucault relies in part on their historic writings to elaborate his notion of 'governmentality'.
2 Being governed through one's freedom is a term that describes one important aspect of 'governmentality', a term developed by Nikolas Rose. During the 1990s Rose's work did a great deal to stimulate Foucaultian governmentality studies in the English-speaking world and beyond, as will be discussed in the next chapter; see for example his book *Powers of Freedom* (1999).
3 For an excellent history of *loi de police* and urban administration, see Napoli (2003). My comments on *loi de justice* versus *loi de police* are based on Napoli's work.

Bibliography

Dean, Mitchell. 1999 [2010]. *Governmentality: Power and Rule in Modern Society*. Los Angeles, CA: Sage.
Foucault, Michel. 1997. *Ethics: Subjectivity and Truth: Essential Works of Michel Foucault 1954–1984, Vol. I*. Edited by Paul Rabinow. Translated by Robert Hurley. New York: New Press.
Foucault, Michel. 2007. *Security, Territory, Population: Lectures at the Collège de France, 1977–1978*. Edited by Michel Senellart. Translated by Graham Burchell. New York: Picador/Palgrave Macmillan.
Napoli, Paolo. 2003. *Naissance de la Police Moderne*. Paris: La Decouverte.
Rose, Nikolas. 1999. *Powers of Freedom: Reframing Political Thought*. Cambridge: Cambridge University Press.

Chapter 5

Governmentality studies in criminology and sociolegal studies: the emergence of 'governmentality' as a paradigm

The 1991 publication of an anthology containing one of Foucault's lectures on 'governmentality' (taken from the series of lectures given at the Collège de France in 1977–78), together with important relevant essays by noted European and British scholars, was an important event in contemporary social science theory (see Foucault 1991, 2007). That Foucault had experimented with the term 'governmentality' was already known in some circles, among other reasons because many people had attended his lectures in person, and others had later travelled to Paris to listen to the available audiotapes and had summarized some ideas in their own publications. But the 1991 volume, entitled *The Foucault Effect: Studies in Governmentality*, can be taken as marking the emergence of 'governmentality studies' amongst English-speaking scholars in a number of different research areas, from the history of statistics to health studies to empirical studies of security.

At that time, the most important place in which researchers familiarized themselves with Foucault's tentative ideas about governmentality and security, and used them in various research projects, was London – specifically a loose group of researchers (including Colin Gordon, Graham Burchell, Peter Miller and Nikolas Rose), many associated with the journal *Ideology and Consciousness*. But *The Foucault Effect* was soon avidly read in Australia and in English Canada, and gained some readers in the US, initially mainly through networks established at Berkeley, where Foucault had resided and given lectures in the early 1980s.

If the book was an immediate success, within critical criminology as in many other fields, it was because within criminology and legal studies, the way towards what quickly came to be called 'governmentality studies' had been already prepared (for more on this see Rose et al. 2006). Around 1990–92, theoretically oriented researchers who had given much thought to Foucault's published books had gone on to reflect on the fact that our contemporary societies cannot be adequately described simply by using terms such as 'discipline' and 'normalization', or even by adding 'biopolitics' to the mix.

To briefly describe the intellectual ground on which governmentality studies quickly took root and flourished, we can select two highly influential articles: one by Australian criminologist Pat O'Malley, published in 1992 but largely written before *The Foucault Effect*; and one whose primary author was South African criminologist Clifford Shearing, a noted policing scholar who had long worked in Canada. (A work of the same time period that also had a significant impact on criminology and sociolegal studies, Nikolas Rose's *Governing the Soul* (1990), should be given considerable credit in any account of governmentality studies; but it is not discussed here because it is less directly concerned with criminological questions.)

Clifford Shearing was motivated to begin thinking about post-disciplinary forms of order and control by an everyday experience – a visit, with his young daughter, to Florida's Disney World. In an article co-authored with Philip Stenning entitled 'From the Panopticon to Disney World', which first appeared in a relatively obscure Canadian book in 1985 but which was later widely read and reprinted, Shearing describes in detail the micromanagement of very large crowds of visitors that the Disney corporation has perfected in its theme parks (Shearing and Stenning 1985). To someone who had read Foucault and had long studied crime control, the way in which Disney World's attractions were arranged and supervised to keep crowds docile despite very long queues suggested that Foucault's well-known argument about the prison as the laboratory of discipline did not suffice to theorize the forms of social control, corporate security and crowd policing utilized in the Disney theme park.

First, Disney does not use specialized police or security forces, but relies rather on the subtler technique of making all personnel, including those in Mickey Mouse and other costumes, responsible for ensuring both safety for visitors and security for the corporation that owns and operates the site. This is remarkably similar to how security is achieved in most workplaces. Most private employers do not have specialized security guards, but instead rely on secretarial and reception staff and other employees to keep an eye on visitors and on other employees as they go about their daily work. Security is thus not hived off to a police force, but is rather embedded in other jobs. The result is that security work becomes invisible; furthermore, security work is accepted by those being policed. As the authors put it:

> A critical consequence of this process of embedding control in other structures is that control becomes consensual ... Thus, adult visitors willingly submit to a variety of devices that increase the flow of consumers through Disney World, such as being corralled on the monorail platform, so as to ensure the safety of their children. Furthermore, while doing so they gratefully acknowledge the concern Disney Productions has for their family, thereby legitimating its authority.
>
> (Shearing and Stenning 1985: 344)

Second, while Foucault's analysis of carceral discipline had argued that surveillance involved the monitoring and examination of individuals, in Disney World surveillance and control are achieved, with great success, without any need for the authorities to know or even see their customers individually. The complex and expensive mechanisms devised by carceral and asylum authorities to probe the souls and reform the bodily conduct of the individuals in their care do not exist in Disney World, or for that matter in much of today's world. Just as city planners and landscape architects change the behaviour of park visitors without preaching to them or chastising them, simply by arranging objects and spaces in patterns that will 'naturally' generate certain patterns of use, so too in Disney World 'every pool, fountain, and flower garden serves both as an aesthetic object and to direct visitors away from, or towards, particular locations' (Shearing and Stenning 1985: 302). Because people think of flowers as beauty items, and they think of aesthetics as quite separate from law and order, people do not notice that the real purpose of a particular flowerpot may well be to prevent them from entering a particular place. A flowerpot is more effective than a large sign reading 'Do not enter'. And if anyone dares to breach the rules – as Shearing's daughter did when she took off her sandals because she had a blister (a not particularly disorderly action that meant she was in contravention of the 'no bare feet' Disney policy) – then compliance will be obtained not by law enforcement measures but by deploying someone who is dressed in a costume to tell the offending visitor that if she chooses to go barefoot she will be thrown out of the theme park. Shearing's daughter, not surprisingly, 'chose' to put her sandal back on when told about the 'no bare feet' policy by a costumed employee, despite the pain of the blister, so as not to lose out on the day's enjoyment. The Disney corporation thus may have paved the way for the airport signs that now tell you that you are not obligated to submit to security searches but that if you refuse to comply with the policy you will be effectively 'choosing' to not board your plane.

Control through architectural and design features; surveillance without personalized discipline; careful management of situations and opportunities rather than of crimes and offenders and so forth – the Disney World example described in 1985 by Shearing and Stenning highlights many of the features of what would later come to be called 'governmentality'.

On his part, Pat O'Malley – then at LaTrobe University in Melbourne, Australia – published an article in a major British social theory journal that sought to further Foucaultian analyses, but similarly showed the limitations of the array of ideas associated with 'discipline': 'Risk, power, and crime prevention' (O'Malley 1992). Drawing on ideas already put forward by noted British criminologist Stan Cohen, O'Malley noted that many if not most crime prevention programmes of the time did not seek to identify 'deviants', much less reform them, but sought simply to minimize opportunities for crime by reshaping the physical environment. Situational crime prevention, the heart of most community safety programmes (both those initiated by police and those initiated by neighbours or by property owners), is an enterprise that can be characterized, in Foucaultian terms, as 'post-disciplinary'. Seeking to govern crime without reforming people or disciplining anyone by acting on opportunities rather than on persons, such programmes, O'Malley suggested, require new theoretical tools. One such tool is what O'Malley called 'prudentialism', a term closely related to what quickly became a widely used word, 'responsibilization'.

Responsibilization is a term drawing attention to the fact that in crime prevention, as in other areas of life, the 1980s and 1990s witnessed a major change whereby ordinary people did indeed come to be responsibilized for their own fate along many different dimensions. O'Malley's pioneering ideas about responsibilization were influenced by his interest in private insurance, pension schemes and actuarial calculations. The shift observed in many countries (including Australia) from universal, state-provided pension plans to the new world of individualized schemes that encourage workers to learn about investment options – with government responsibility being limited to various fiscal measures to incentivize different forms of saving (education savings plans, individual retirement plans, home ownership incentives, etc.) – was not an isolated phenomenon limited to the field of retirement pensions. In keeping with Foucault's methodological insight about the way in which governance inventions travel easily from one field to another, the individualization of risk management and the responsibilization of ordinary employees that came to the fore in the field of personal finance also became visible at around the same time in the field of crime and crime prevention. The 1970s was a decade of relatively high crime compared to today and compared to earlier decades, and police forces as well as community groups developed new programmes that relied greatly on exhorting home owners to become vigilant and invest in home security systems. Such programmes treat crime as a personal risk rather than as a problem for the state to solve.

In that 1992 article, O'Malley noted that police officers' response to home burglaries had started to focus more on giving advice to property owners and less on the state's responsibility to apprehend and punish criminals. In the corporate sector too, companies had little interest in identifying which employees might possibly steal corporate property; instead, they hired consultants to show them how to reorganize furniture and people so as to generally lower the opportunities for crime. Such situational crime prevention refuses to divide the workforce or the population into groups such as the well-behaved and the deviant. The techniques treat everyone in exactly the same way – as a rational-choice actor who may well pilfer company goods if it is easy to get away with it, but will not commit crimes if the chances of being observed and caught are significant.

In a way, the situational crime prevention that boomed in the era of 'broken windows' (the 1980s) could be said to return criminology to its classical Beccarian origins. As is well known, the late eighteenth-century thinker Cesare Beccaria believed that, whatever the real differences between people may be, the criminal justice system should ignore those differences; it should be constructed as a perfectly rational machine in which each particular crime is outweighed by just enough punishment to deter the hypothetical rational-choice average person from committing it. But, looked at from a Foucaultian perspective, situational crime prevention is not exactly a return to late eighteenth-century classical criminology. Techniques such as police giving advice on how to secure one's back door, or Disney characters being deployed to ensure that no visitors step off the officially designed paths or contravene any Disney policies, reflect not so much the optimist rationalism of Beccaria's Enlightenment, but rather a new, postmodern and arguably neoliberal cynicism towards the welfare state – a disenchantment with the centralized planning and universal social programmes ideals of the postwar period.

The same neoliberal scepticism towards state planning and state law can be discerned in the proliferation of private or semi-private security forces; civil society-led crime prevention efforts; and the emergence of what some scholars have now called 'networks' of security provision – as argued for example by Oxford criminologist Ian Loader in an article that, while not overtly based on Foucault's work, puts to use most of the governmentality-related themes discussed in this chapter (Loader 2000). And the same trends are detectable in the enthusiasm for public-private partnerships that has been documented in Brazilian correctional programmes (Macaulay 2013)

Having given a sense of some of the ideas about trends in crime control that were, even before the publication of any of Foucault's governmentality lectures, indicating a need to go beyond Foucault's analysis of discipline, the rest of this chapter will draw on a very small sample of the large governmentality literature in criminology and sociolegal studies in such a way as to highlight key notions and themes.

Responsibilization

As just mentioned, O'Malley's key article on risk and crime prevention highlighted the way in which contemporary programmes responsibilize citizens, especially home owners, for crime risks. But responsibilization is not limited to that context. Another context in which it was becoming increasingly popular around the same time (late 1980s and early 1990s) was that of therapeutic and other problem-solving courts. Such courts can be extremely coercive, for instance sending someone back to remand detention if their urine test suggests they used drugs even once; but the premise of such programmes is that the offenders are not being coercively punished, but are simply being encouraged to do what is assumed they want to do – that is, get clean and get better. Psychiatrists are rarely made available, and to that extent programmes like drug treatment courts are not classic disciplinary strategies. Instead, these courts rely on group therapy, peer support and some more or less common sense-based counselling by people who do have some training but are not about to engage in long-term 'disciplinary' work on an individual's mind/soul.

The new brand of governmentality criminologists soon began to note that the people who are selected for such contemporary programmes as drug treatment courts are more likely to be governed through their own freedom, through their desire to be 'free' from substance addiction, than to be told (as might have been the case in the 1950s) that they are 'deviants'. Aligning the interests and desires of the people being governed with the aims of the authorities – in drug treatment court as in Disney World – is a key feature of the contemporary style of governance known as governmentality.

Similarly, some prison programmes (especially in institutions for women or young offenders) that proceed on the basis that prisoners are not a deviant group but are merely ordinary people who have made the wrong choices, and who need the opportunity to reflect and be supported in making the 'right' life choices, can also be said to be part of a governmentality-style approach to prisons. Decades ago prisoners were often taught a trade. Today, it is more likely that, instead of learning a definite trade, prisoners will be offered an 'opportunity' to participate in a generic 'life skills' course where they are exhorted to exercise their right – indeed their duty – to make life choices.

This approach (involving responsibilization and governing people through their very desire for autonomy and freedom) has strong parallels in other fields. In medical care, for example, the old-fashioned doctor who simply declared that the patient needs to have this particular operation right away has given way to the 'responsibilizing' practitioner. Such a practitioner does not impose particular views in a top-down, I know what's good for you fashion. Instead, such a personage informs patients about the risks or this versus that course of action, emphasizing that the treatment must be the patient's informed choice. In the medical context responsibilization may feel more like a burden than a benefit to the person whose body is at stake, especially in the case of complex, multiple-speciality situations that ordinary people cannot properly evaluate; but the trend today in primary health care is indeed to emphasize responsibilization and informed choice. The fact that it is often very difficult for ordinary people to gather and evaluate the relevant data (in health care as in financial planning) seems to have caused no dent in the general enthusiasm for this way of governing people and institutions.

Managing risks through data

As discussed in Chapter 2, disciplinary strategies seek to reform behaviour, either in particular individuals (e.g. through religious indoctrination or psychiatric treatment) or in a particular population, as when students in a particular city or a school board are forced to wear the same uniforms.

One of the features of governmentality is that the focus shifts from actual behaviour change in the present to the management of future risks. Of course the two strategies can and often do go together; in criminal justice as in the school system or in private corporations, there is often a division of labour whereby some personnel do the disciplining, face to face, while others sit in the back offices collecting data and attempting to predict the future on the basis of past data ('predictive policing' is the latest trend in this regard). It is important to note that not all risks are calculable: whether I will be struck by lightning as I go home from work today is a risk that cannot be in any serious way managed beforehand through data collection (except perhaps through prayer, which is not the kind of activity that Foucaultian analysis is well placed to appreciate). But many other more common risks are indeed calculable to some extent, and risk calculations are at the heart of governmentality.

The link between the desire to manage risks – calculable risks, that is – and the gathering of information in the specific form of 'data' is thus very strong. Therefore, what Foucault first called 'security' and then 'governmentality' is characterized by authorities' preference for what is now called 'big data'. This can be illustrated by using a perhaps trivial example. If one looks up a particular business on Google, one now often sees a chart (without asking for it – it simply appears on the bottom of one's screen) that indicates, hour by hour, how busy the place is, from opening to closing. This is a perfect example of governmentality in action. Google, the impartial data aggregator par excellence, does not tell you whether you should go to the store at all; does not judge if their products are better than a competitor's; and does not tell you when to go to shop or get a service. Google does not discipline its users; and neither does it have any mechanism for punishing users who do 'the wrong thing' (insofar as there is any right and wrong in the Google universe, which is not very far). Google simply gives you information that may be useful in exercising your free will – or at least that is how it appears. In fact, of course, providing data showing how busy an office or shop is at particular times of the day must be intended to change consumer behaviour by quietly encouraging those whose time is flexible to go at less busy times and avoid the rush hours. But in taking the information into account when planning their errands, customers will no doubt feel that they are exercising freedom of choice – a freedom that is enabled and powered by information, by neutral, objective, factual information. It will not occur to many patrons to think about who might be paying to collect and aggregate and then display, in convenient graph form, the information in question. And few consumers will stop to think that it is very much in the interests of the business in question to divulge to Google and thus publicize the customer data broken down by hours of operation so as to encourage people to distribute themselves more evenly throughout the day. People will appear to be acting out of pure, individual free choice in showing up at a time that the graph shows to be less busy. A Foucaultian analysis would say that while that type of freedom is by no means false or illusory, since the consumers are indeed free to go at the busiest time if they so choose and there is no punishment for doing so, their behaviour is certainly not 'free' in the sense of undetermined.

It is important to note, for the purposes of contrasting governmentality with other strategies of power/knowledge, that in the Google business time-chart case, as in health care and financial planning contexts, the exercise of what may feel like free individual choice is mediated by data collected and organized by entities that are not particularly interested in our freedom, but are rather keen on maximizing their profits by selling products that in turn maximize the efficiency of their customers' own enterprises. The alignment of our desire for freedom with those data-gathering entities' desire for market share is thus one that happens without anyone willing it.

Power is thus not necessarily a matter of conspiracies and plans. Power is sometimes produced through the coming together of different projects and different information needs. That all knowledge, including apparently value-free data such as the number of customers per hour, is power is of course a key

Foucaultian insight, as discussed in Chapter 1. But neither knowledge nor power exists in general, as also explained in Chapter 1; they only exist in particular forms. Knowledge is always presented in particular formats. In the case of the Google business time chart, here knowledge is presented in the form of quantitative data – rather than, say, as a journalistic, qualitative, dramatic description of an office or a shop that is besieged by people at 9 am and then becomes almost empty by 11 am. Knowledge is power, in general; data gathering, however, is the particular type of knowledge exercise that tends to favour the particular form of power known as governmentality.

Along these lines, in the criminal justice research realm, we now have countless studies of how authorities use data to generate risk assessment scales and other quantitative tools to rate, rank, organize and distribute offenders and prisoners. It should be acknowledged that most of these studies are influenced not only by Foucault but also by an overlapping literature on risk and risk management that has a somewhat different, non-Foucaultian provenance, a complex literature that is not within the scope of this book. For present purposes it suffices to say that while Foucault himself did not enter into the details of various risk management tools and risk techniques, his studies of the rise of governmentality in modern Europe did draw attention to the important role played in the emergence of modern, liberal forms of power by the rise not only of knowledge in general but of knowledge in the specific form of data. And in the Foucaultian frame, there is a close connection between the popularity of data on the one hand, and the rise of risk management and risk minimization on the other (although some forms of disciplinary normalization, such as those based on IQ and other aptitude tests, also require data to support them).

Having covered responsibilization and risk management through data, we can now go on to two other themes that recur very frequently in the governmentality literature. The first concerns a certain quiet shift from governing persons directly (as school discipline or prison discipline does) to governing indirectly by rearranging space – a trend already discussed above in the context of situational crime prevention.

Governing through space

The rise and the strengthening of individual rights against the state, for example in the context of policing and the rights of the accused, has meant that for legal reasons it is more difficult now to govern persons coercively in a direct manner. In many jurisdictions it is now unconstitutional to simply name a category of person (prostitute, vagrant, beggar) and put a criminal or quasi-criminal label on that type of person. To put it differently, status offences have to a large extent been relegated to the dustbin of legal history. As a response, not surprisingly, many jurisdictions (especially municipalities, which have always had great powers to micromanage both public space and private real estate, but few if any powers to govern persons coercively) have made creative use of their powers to govern space in order to essentially target the usual suspects. Today, vagrancy statutes have been largely abolished; and yet a host of regulations have been put in place, such as bylaws stating that it is illegal to camp overnight, drink alcoholic beverages, or even just remain in the park after sundown, however orderly one might be. It is perfectly obvious that it is homeless people or youth who do not have private space at home who are the ones likely to be charged with breaches of such park use rules; but nevertheless those rules will not be seen by courts as constitutionally invalid because they target a vulnerable group, since the letter of the law forbids everyone, not just a particular group, from using the park as a kind of home.

Developments in constitutional law, therefore, have greatly encouraged a shift from the direct governance of types of people to the indirect governance of types of people by the implementation of rules about using spaces at particular times in particular ways, rules that appear to be neutral as to persons.

But whether the shift to 'governing through space' is legally motivated or not, the fact is that what some scholars call 'spatial governmentality' has experienced a boom (see for example Beckett and Herbert 2008 and Merry 2001). From ordinances in US cities that prohibit not only sleeping but even sitting or lying down on sidewalks, to the myriad rules of civil behaviour that are imposed in the quasi-public, quasi-private spaces of sociability that are shopping malls, contemporary cities have generated veritable mountains of regulations that govern people and activities through spatio-temporally specific rules.

The same trend towards spatial governmentality is also visible in certain criminal justice fields, especially probation and parole. It is now very common for minor offenders, if granted bail, to be given a map of the city that outlines the 'red' zone that they are not allowed to enter. The theory is that 'criminals' associate with other criminals in particular places, with negative results for the respectable community, and that banning offenders from areas that have been associated either with their particular past crimes or with other people's crimes is a good crime-prevention measure. That may be true in some cases; but many critical criminologists have shown that spatial restrictions are over-used and often have the negative effect of preventing people from accessing either social services or friends and relatives who might help and support law-abiding behaviour. (Many social services are indeed located in 'criminogenic' areas of cities.)

Whether used wisely or used in an overly punitive or simply dysfunctional manner, the point here is that spatial restrictions imposed on offenders can be seen as part of a larger move away from governing persons directly through disciplinary mechanisms and towards governing problems and persons impersonally, through spatial measures. Governmentality, as outlined in Chapter 4, is Foucault's word for a way of governing that is, or at least tries to be, impersonal and data-driven, and which is more interested in controlling and managing the future (by governing risks) than in either punishing anyone for acts committed in the past or in micromanaging bodies and souls to produce normalized individuals. Spatial governmentality, then, while clearly visible in many criminal justice contexts, is a much broader phenomenon.

Community

There are many other themes and analytical terms that have been identified in the governmentality literature, but one that has particular relevance to legal and criminological contexts is what has been described as a shift from 'the state' to 'the community'. As Nikolas Rose points out, in previous eras 'community' was a term designating an organic, pre-political entity that predates law and predates the state and remains in some fundamental ways opposed to the state. But today community has firmly lodged itself within the state – as in mandated police–community partnerships or state officials whose jobs are described as 'community development officers' (Rose 1999: 174–9). Community, in the world of governmentality, cannot be left to grow organically on its own; community requires investigation, data collection (as in 'community profiles' of neighbourhoods, generated by means of census data) and even experts in 'empowering' the communities in question. To put it differently, the state now often governs *through* community.

Community, then, is a term that might have once denoted spontaneous and largely informal interactions between neighbours or other private citizens, but that today, while still enjoying the halo effect of the mythical village-like, bottom-up community, has become both a social space to be governed and a vehicle to govern other things. An excellent example is the proliferation, in the US, of community notification laws requiring that neighbours within a certain area be informed if a sex offender released from prison is slated to live in their area. One could say that these measures are state responses to populist, community-based concerns about the safety of children – and that would not be untrue. But it would also be true to note that it is the laws themselves that artificially create a particular 'community', demarcating that community by literally drawing lines around a space that might not otherwise hold much by way of communal life. The sum of householders who live less than a certain number of metres from a particular address is unlikely to actually be a community in the sociological sense.

So 'community' is operationalized and even brought into existence by state law, in a way that resonates strongly with the analysis given above of responsibilization. 'Community', in Rose's influential analysis, becomes a term used to govern all manner of things that were perhaps not quite so governed before, or which may not even have existed before:

> Rather, in the institution of community, a sector is brought into existence whose vectors and forces can be mobilized,

> enrolled, deployed in novel programmes and techniques which encourage and harness active practices of self-management and identity construction, of personal ethics and collective allegiances. I term this *government through community*.
>
> (Rose 1999: 176)

Sometimes 'community' is used simply as a synonym for 'neighbourhood'. In these cases, talk about community is often linked to a rejection of city-wide or regional planning, and goes hand in hand with the contemporary tendency of both city officials and citizen activists to believe that civic life is micro-local and that urban design should focus on one little space at time a – a park, an intersection, perhaps a block or at most a couple of blocks.

But community is not always linked to particular houses and streets. People can also be described as belonging to the Italian community, the gay/lesbian community, even the breast cancer community. In those cases, bottom-up democratic citizenship and advocacy emerge to voice the concerns of a group that shares some interests. But that type of community also becomes, inevitably, something that is both itself governed and that becomes a vehicle for various authorities, corporate or state-based, to govern us *through* community. For example, our votes may be solicited for an upcoming election on the grounds that we belong to this or that ethnic or other minority community; and the subsequent electoral process will then have the effect of reifying the 'community' in question – as when people say candidate X has the Muslim vote or the gay/lesbian vote locked up, as if people's politics were wholly determined by one particular type of belonging. And today's data analytics allows pollsters and those who work for candidates to operationalize and subdivide different 'communities' with greater and greater statistical sophistication.

The popularity of 'community' talk, then, is one site on which we can see the usefulness of Foucault's emphasis on always documenting and noting less obvious flows of power, even in situations and contexts that may also, at the same time, be sites for freedom and self-determination.

In general, the rich governmentality studies literature has drawn our attention to relatively new techniques of governance that tend to govern *through* rather than *against* our desire for freedom; that are more impersonal than either discipline or sovereign punishment; and that concern themselves more with managing future risks than with imposing moral codes or probing deeply into the inner self. In the world of governmentality we are neither free nor unfree; or, perhaps better, we are simultaneously more free than in other contexts but are also less free in that our very desire for freedom is at least to some extent produced by techniques such as responsibilization and governing through community.

Bibliography

Becket, Katherine and Steve Herbert. 2008. 'Dealing with Disorder: Social Control in the Post-Industrial City.' *Theoretical Criminology* 12 (1): 5–30.

Foucault, Michel. 1991. *The Foucault Effect: Studies in Governmentality: with Two Lectures by and an Interview with Michel Foucault*. Edited by Graham Burchell, Colin Gordon, and Peter Miller. Chicago, IL: University of Chicago Press.

Foucault, Michel. 2007. *Security, Territory, Population: Lectures at the Collège de France, 1977–1978*. Edited by Michel Senellart. Translated by Graham Burchell. New York: Picador/Palgrave Macmillan.

Loader, Ian. 2000. 'Plural Policing and Democratic Governance.' *Social and Legal Studies* 9(3): 323–345.

Macaulay, Fiona. 2013. 'Modes of Prison Administration, Control and Governmentality in Latin America.' *Conflict, Security and Development* 13(4): 361–392.

Merry, Sally Engle. 2001. 'Spatial Governmentality and the New Urban Social Order: Controlling Gender Violence through Law.' *American Anthropologist* 163(1): 16–29.

O'Malley, Pat. 1992. 'Risk, Power and Crime Prevention.' *Economy and Society* 21(3): 252–275.

Rose, Nikolas. 1990. *Governing the Soul: The Shaping of the Private Self*. London, New York: Routledge.

Rose, Nikolas. 1999. *Powers of Freedom: Reframing Political Thought*. Cambridge: Cambridge University Press.

Rose, Nikolas, Pat O'Malley, and Mariana Valverde. 2006. 'Governmentality.' *Annual Review of Law and Social Science* 2(1): 83–104.

Shearing, Clifford and Philip Stenning. 1985. 'From the Panopticon to Disney World: the Development of Discipline,' in Anthony N. Doob and Edward L. Greenspan, eds, *Perspectives in Criminal Law: Essays in Honour of John LL.J. Edwards*. Aurora, Ont.: Canada Law Books, pp. 336–349.

Chapter 6

The punitive society

The 1972–73 lectures at the Collège de France given under the overall title *The Punitive Society* were published in English only in 2015. This very belatedly published volume will have a significant impact on our understanding of Foucault's work on punishment and forms of power. The lectures contain some material that was revised and published two years later in *Discipline and Punish* (1979); but reading the recently published lectures shows that a great deal was left on the cutting-room floor. In addition, it is very enlightening for today's scholars to see, in the lectures, that Foucault presented a wide variety of analyses of various historical events and texts relevant to questions of punishment and discipline over the course of eight weeks, deciding only at the very end of the lecture series that the central term in his analysis of the genealogy of punishment should be 'discipline'.

Thus, both because the recently published volume gives us new insights into Foucault's intellectual processes and because of the intrinsic interest of many ideas relevant to criminology that were central for the lectures but that disappeared from the eventual book, it is worth devoting this chapter to that lecture series.

Foucault delivered the lectures just after a period of two years during which he spent an inordinate amount of time and energy on prison-related activism. As discussed in Chapter 2, while many other intellectuals of the time had a great deal of youthful activist experience – with membership in various European communist parties being a common experience for that generation – Foucault had very little by way of activist credentials. It was only when he started to take an interest in imprisonment issues that Foucault changed his habits and got involved in front-line activism. Bernard Harcourt points out in the brief but superbly researched 'Course context' commentary, included in the *Punitive Society* volume, that Foucault and his fellow activists may not have been able to gain access to French prisons, but that Foucault did visit New York state's Attica prison in 1972, a few months after the famous riot that culminated in the death of 29 prisoners and 10 correctional officers. Although French prisons also experienced revolts around this time (as was the case in other countries as well), with Foucault and his small group of activist comrades doing support work for the prisoners, it may be that the Black Panthers and other highly politicized prison activists in the US were more important in motivating Foucault's intellectual work on punishment than has previously been thought (see Foucault 2015: 265–9).

Foucault's 1971–72 prison activism had been designed as time-limited. Once that political work had achieved its modest aim, which was to allow prisoners themselves to explain prison conditions to the public, and prisoners' associations had been established in France, the group that Foucault and his partner Daniel Defert founded (Groupe d'Information sur les Prisons, GIP) was disbanded, a few weeks before the first of the lectures under review was given (see Chapter 2). There was also a major change in the central government, as the long-reigning right-wing party was replaced by the Socialist Party, with activists placing great hopes on socialist-appointed ministers and justice personnel. Whatever the exact reasons, by the time he began the lectures (in January 1973) Foucault seems to have been in a more scholarly and less activist phase of his work on imprisonment and punishment.

But there had not been much time to reflect on the activism of 1971–72. My own impression from reading the lectures is that even though Foucault had been immersed in historical research on prisons and punishment throughout, since activism was not for him a replacement for doing research, his ideas were still very much in process when he started the lectures. If the answers had not yet gelled, however, the questions Foucault was asking had been clear for some time, and indeed are also the same questions underlying *Discipline and Punish*. Asking why the penitentiary, an institution that failed to meet its stated purpose from the start, quickly became 'best practice' in criminal punishment and persisted into the present led Foucault to an evolving analysis of the actual (as opposed to intended) effects furthered by the proliferation of penitentiaries and reformatories. As explained in detail in Chapter 2, the techniques perfected in penitentiaries (surveillance, hierarchical observation, examinations and normalization) were shown in Foucault's historically based analysis to serve to create not so much rehabilitated prisoners as a whole broader society – a 'disciplinary' society. And, to reiterate another key point made in Chapter 2, what makes Foucault's account of 'the birth of the prison' relevant well outside criminology is that Foucault argued that disciplinary projects may have been most easily put in place in correctional institution contexts, but that, in less total form, disciplinary techniques and rationalities pervade and give shape to modern social organization – from the kindergarten to the welfare office, from corporate headquarters buildings to refugee camps.

While readers familiar with *Discipline and Punish* would expect 'discipline' to have also been the central term in the 1973 lectures, in fact in this set of lectures discipline only emerges as a key concept towards the end. A number of practices discussed in the later book under the term 'discipline' appear in the lectures, but without that label being used. Thus, in this chapter we will be peering into Foucault's thinking process, as it were, and documenting some of the steps along the somewhat uneven road that eventually led to 'discipline', a term that in the better-known book published in 1975 was presented as fully formed even in the opening pages. Along the way we will also discuss important ideas that were left out of the book and are thus not covered in Chapter 2. One such group of ideas is found in Foucault's reflexive comments on terms prevalent among left-wing intellectuals in the early 1970s: 'exclusion' and 'transgression'.

The limits of the 1968 generation's focus on 'exclusion' and 'transgression'

The more or less anarchist spirit of the worker and student uprisings that shook France and other countries in 1968–70 made much use of the rather abstract notions of 'exclusion' and 'transgression' (the latter term being especially associated with the writer Georges Bataille). By contrast to Marxism's focus on ownership of the means of production, exclusion was – and remains – a term overcoming or subsuming the differences not only between class, race, gender, nationality, etc., but also between the process of socio-economic marginalization on the one hand and the processes of cultural and moral regulation on the other.

Denunciations of exclusion in general, common amongst the *soixante-huitards* (the generation of 1968), were often followed by more or less romantic calls for 'transgression'. In his work of the mid and late 1960s, Foucault largely went along with this framework.[1] Soon after 1968, however, he began to question the utility of such abstract notions. But although abstract notions about exclusion and transgression recede far into the background in his later work, giving way to concrete analyses of particular forms of power embedded in particular governing assemblages, up until the publication of these lectures on the 'punitive society' we had no explanation of how Foucault became disenchanted with the 1968 naïve notion that all authority should be contested and that all transgressions are creative. We now have this auto-critique in the very first lecture, where Foucault wonders whether an abstract attitude of refusal and resistance might not be in fact unwittingly reinforcing the claims and self-images put forward by the very authorities being denounced and refused.

> I think that the notions of exclusion and transgression should now be considered as instruments that were important historically: for a given period they were critical reversers in the sphere of juridical, political, and moral representations; but these reversers remain pegged to the general system of representations against which they are turned.
>
> (Foucault 2015: 6)

Foucault goes on:

> It seems to me that the directions indicated by the analyses conducted in terms of exclusion and transgression should be

> pursued in new dimensions in which it is no longer a question of the law, the rule, the representation, but of power rather than the law.
>
> (Foucault 2015: 6)

'Law' here has an ambiguous meaning, since Lacanian psychoanalysis, then in vogue in France, used the term 'law' not in the legal sense but to refer to the general structure of social authority. But be that as it may, it is clear Foucault is beginning to think about how to get beyond purely negative denunciations of the force of law and/or the exclusions of bourgeois society and instead try to think more concretely and historically about different forms of power which emerged independently of law.

And, following his own advice in sidelining the binary opposition of authority or law versus transgression, Foucault turns away from the kind of philosophical generalizations about punishment that are the bread and butter of criminal-law theory. Instead, he gives a brief comment on the widely different forms that criminal punishment has taken over the centuries. These practices include not only scarring the body, confinement and expulsion from the community but also – an important penal sanction that remained unmentioned in *Discipline and Punish* – imposing fines (Foucault 2015: 7).

Pat O'Malley (2009) has argued that progressive criminologists' exclusive focus on imprisonment and its penumbra (probation, parole) and the consequent neglect of the fine – the most common form of punishment – has created theoretical as well as empirical distortions. In this lecture Foucault does not go on to discuss fines in detail; but he opens up interesting avenues for research as he notes that fines are ubiquitous because they can serve different purposes, depending on the overall logic of the particular punishment assemblage in which they exist (Foucault 2015: 8–9). The exclusion of the comments about fines from *Discipline and Punish* was quite unfortunate, in retrospect, since it seems to have had the effect of reinforcing criminology's tendency to be obsessed with imprisonment, even in regard to times and places where that is not the primary form of state punishment.

But if abstract exclusion and equally abstract transgression are said to be deficient, or at any rate limited, and if using such terms obscures a whole range of important phenomena (such as the importance and varied functions of fines), what frame can be used instead to think about power and authority? Addressing this question brings Foucault to a lengthy discussion of 'civil war' as the default setting of social relations, a discussion also wholly missing from *Discipline and Punish*.

Civil war as the default setting for social relations – and as the frame for punishment

In the second part of the first lecture (January 3, 1973), Foucault argues that concrete forms of punitiveness should not be used as data used to 'reconstruct the set of juridical and moral representations that are supposed to support and justify these penal practices' (2015: 12). That is of course what is done in ordinary criminal law teaching, especially criminal law theory. Instead, Foucault argues that penal practices are best regarded as 'tactics' deployed in the constant 'play of conflicts' that makes up social relations generally.

That Foucault falls within what sociology would call a 'conflict perspective' is hardly news; but what is interesting here is that Foucault speaks not merely about conflict, but specifically about civil war. Civil war, here, constitutes what Foucaultian scholars would call a general diagram of power, but it is said to apply specifically to penality: 'it is the notion of *civil war* that must be put at the heart of all of these analyses of penality' (ibid.: 13, emphasis in original). This statement (which is not found in *Discipline and Punish*) clearly places Foucault well outside the liberal mainstream. Far from seeing state punishment as 'paying your dues to society', Foucault presents a rather cynical view whereby punishment appears as the legalization of violence committed by the powerful against the powerless, against those members of the lower orders who have been criminalized.

The civil war frame (which clearly is meant to include all manner of 'cold' civil wars between the rich and powerful on the one hand and the disentitled on the other) is theoretically useful in that it allows Foucault to distance himself from the main three perspectives used then (and now) to theorize – and justify – the coercive power of the state. First, and most explicitly developed, a contrast is drawn with social contract theory. Social contract thought begins with the premise that the default setting for human relations is individualist competition, and goes on to argue that the contradictions of the 'state of nature' (such as the anarchy inherent in individuals taking the law into their own hands) necessarily lead to a 'social contract', a horizontal agreement to limit individualism and invest a central authority with the sole power to issue laws and punish wrongdoers. For social contract theory, the only two 'normal' states of political affairs are thus a lawless pre-political society in which the family is the only organized social form on the one hand (the state of nature); and, on the other hand, a proper 'commonwealth' in which sovereignty has been achieved and is constantly defended and justified. Even those social contract theorists who do not share Hobbes' cynicism about human nature (Rousseau is mentioned, though without any explicit differentiation from Hobbes) are covered by Foucault's critique, since they too see civil war as a contingent and disastrous event – 'civil war is the accident, the abnormality' (Foucault 2015: 13). Inspired perhaps by Nietzsche, Foucault's musings on civil war as the norm rather than the exception is meant to disrupt the conventional liberal view that there are only two normal human conditions: the state of nature; and the liberal, consensually produced state that 'naturally' arises to resolve the chaos and violence that pervades the state of nature.

Thus, taking civil war as the default setting displaces and disrupts the assumptions of contract theories, clearly. But it also displaces and disrupts Durkheimian theories of punishment and social cohesion, as Foucault outlines in notes for the lecture for which he did not have time in the oral presentation. Punishment, Foucault wrote in his notes, is best seen as one of the tools by which one group dominates or controls another. Clearly aiming at Durkheim, Foucault then proceeds to cast aspersions on the notion that punishment is the expression of 'society as a whole, en masse, in obscure consensus' (ibid.: 14, footnote).

The civil war trope may well have been borrowed from Nietzsche; though in Nietzsche such discussions often end by denouncing 'weak' or 'slavish' groups or peoples, and praising conduct that is 'Dionysian', virile and strong – and Foucault certainly does not follow Nietzsche there. In Foucault's work the civil war trope seems to play mainly a critical function. That is, there is no strong claim that all social relations are at bottom forms of civil war. Rather, the argument (as I see it) is that it is more useful to emphasize the deep conflicts between the powerful and the subordinate than it is to promote ideas about how state punishment is either something we all implicitly agreed to when 'joining' political society (in the social contract framing) or else something that (in Durkheim's view) helps societies restore their social cohesion, as the passion shown in denouncing and punishing malefactors acts to renew the basic 'mechanical' solidarity that even the most advanced societies need to maintain.

Having critiqued both social contract theory and Durkheimian functionalism by invoking civil war, what Foucault does not need to tell his audience (given that it was 1973 and that he was speaking in Paris) is that the civil war frame also displaces 'class struggle', then the dominant frame in left-wing social and political theory.

In the last lecture (March 28), in which Foucault finally presents a fairly coherent critical discussion of Marxism (despite having frequently used Marxist language in the earlier lectures), the audience heard that 'power is never entirely on one side … power is not monolithic' (Foucault 2015: 228). This, as volume editor Bernard Harcourt notes, would have been heard as a direct critique of Louis Althusser's version of Marxism in particular and Marxist views about 'the bourgeois state' in general. Of course these remarks about power being fluid and dispersed rather than static and monolithic are familiar from *Discipline and Punish*. But what is thus new in these lectures is the invocation of civil war: 'Power should not be assimilated to a wealth possessed by some; it is a permanent strategy that should be thought of against the background of civil war' (ibid.: 228–9).

The punitive society or the disciplinary society?

As briefly mentioned at the outset, the notion of 'discipline' emerges clearly only in the last two lectures of the series. As we turn the pages, we see the thought process that over the eight weeks of the lectures led to the well-known 'disciplinary' criminological revolution – or, more accurately, one can see the portion of Foucault's intellectual production process that he chose to make visible, or rather audible. In keeping with what I would argue is a general tendency to minimize or paper over changes in his own intellectual direction, Foucault claims, towards the end of the lecture series, that what he initially called 'punitiveness' and 'the punitive society' is actually synonymous with what he now wants to call 'the disciplinary system' (Foucault 2015: 231).

Why would he suddenly shift to the language of 'discipline'? There is no explicit explanation given; but one obvious virtue of the term 'discipline' is that it clearly zooms out from penality and state punishments to encompass a variety of larger social processes. It would have been possible to retain the word 'punitiveness' and simply insist on an idiosyncratic definition; in the later book, Foucault could have chosen to retain the 1973 meaning of 'punitiveness' and proceeded to document the micro-punitive practices of workplaces and households. But the fact is that the term 'punitiveness' (unlike 'discipline') is difficult to detach from the realm of criminal law and from the sphere of the state. Perhaps for that reason, in a brief discussion that has no parallel or even faint echo in *Discipline and Punish*, the term 'discipline' is deployed to simultaneously critique both Althusser's notion that the nuclear family is an ideological apparatus of the state and Friedrich Engels' opposing, pro-feminist view that it is the rise of the property-owning family that leads to the bourgeois state. Without naming names, Foucault tells his audience (which would have been familiar with these intra-Marxist debates) that:

> Really, it matters little whether the family reproduces the State or the other way around. The family and the State function in relation to each other, by relying on each other, possibly confronting each other, in a system of power that, in a society like ours, may be characterized as disciplinary in a homogenous way.
>
> (Foucault 2015: 230–31)

Then, Foucault declares: 'Where was I wanting to go [with the lectures]? I wanted to analyze a certain system of power: disciplinary power. It seemed to me, in fact, that we live in a society of disciplinary power' (ibid.: 237).

In my view it is important for us now to note that in his oral presentation Foucault did not acknowledge that the term 'discipline' had actually played little or no role at the beginning of the lecture series. The shift from punitiveness to discipline is explicitly noted in the manuscript notes, helpfully included by Harcourt in the volume, which state that his aim in the lectures was 'the analysis of the form of power I have called punitive, which it would be better to call disciplinary' (ibid.: 37, footnote). But that was not said out loud; and, as just mentioned, even in the handwritten notes Foucault gives no clear detailed explanation of the reasons for the shift in language. Thus, audience members present at the last two lectures who had not been present at the start, or who did not pay much attention to the title of the series, would not have clearly seen that 'disciplinary power' was an after-the-fact label for what had been previously described as 'the punitive society'.

The shift – insofar as there is one – from punitiveness to disciplinarity is particularly intriguing for English-speaking readers, given that the book *Surveiller et Punir* had as its English title *Discipline and Punish*, a title that does not encourage thinking of punishing and disciplining as coterminous. Furthermore, English-speaking criminologists who ponder the significance of Foucault's belated use of 'discipline' in lectures that were collectively entitled 'the punitive society' will have to grapple with the fact that in *Discipline and Punish* 'punitiveness' still appears, but (mainly) in a re-scaled form: the book has a section entitled 'The punitive city'. This section describes neither the penitentiary, nor confinement, nor criminal law. Rather, it covers a very historically specific and somewhat marginal innovation in punishment, namely, some early nineteenth-century experiments in public displays (mini-theatres, as Foucault puts it) of legal punishment. A number of European social reformers wanted to use public displays of convicts performing useful labour (with the labour often bearing a direct relationship to the specific offence) as mini-theatres of citizenship. In many cases the rather elaborate plans for having convicts perform this or that type of labour in public view were not carried out; but the point is that 'the punitive city' is Foucault's name for all the highly symbolic practices of punishment that were meant to educate the public about the meaning of specific crimes and the specific guilt of different criminals.

Thus, as Foucault went on to streamline the book manuscript by focusing his account on 'the birth of the prison', rather than trying to write a fuller and more systematic genealogy of modern punishment (as had been envisaged in the first few 1973 lectures), 'punitiveness' was no longer the general term used to describe methods for governing the bodies and souls of the 'dangerous classes'. In *Discipline and Punish*, as just mentioned, the section 'the punitive city' has a narrower meaning. It describes a number of largely unsuccessful projects promoting the public display of convicts as object lessons to normalize and educate the law-abiding. It is very intriguing that this semiotic experiment in criminal justice is specifically said to belong to the scale of 'the city', perhaps because only cities contained the crowds for whose edification the punishments were made public. How 'the punitive city' of the book squares with the state-level more generalized punitiveness of the lectures is not immediately obvious, however. All that is clear is that 'the punitive city' section of *Discipline and Punish* is only a remnant or a small slice of the larger analysis of punitiveness presented in the lectures.

Let us now move on to a (related) theme that figures very largely in these lectures but was largely cut out of the later book, and which reflects Foucault's deep reading of the then lively field of nineteenth-century working-class history: the constitutive role of moral regulation in the formation of European working classes.

Working-class 'dissipation' as resistance to capitalism

As feminists have pointed out repeatedly, Marx's own work was tremendously sophisticated in its critique of capitalist economic relations; but in regard to domestic organization and gender relations Marx did little or nothing to challenge the status quo.

That socialism would be taken up by respectable men heading up respectable families was simply assumed by Marx himself and by the vast majority of his fellow communists. The competing anti-capitalist critique developed by anarchists (mainly in Russia, Spain and Italy) from the 1870s onward was more suited to a critique of bourgeois moral and family values; but neither anarchism nor the isolated socialist-feminist voices that emerged during the Russian revolution (and later, during the Spanish Civil War of the 1930s) survived into the post-World War II Cold War world. The communist movement of the Cold War era was not interested in anything like a gender or sexual revolution, and saw 'immoral' behaviour found amongst urban underclasses as politically suspicious.

In keeping with Marx's own moralistic comments about the 'lumpenproletariat' (literally, garbage proletariat, meaning the urban underclass), the communist parties that were powerful in many European countries in the Cold War era assumed that the revolutionary working class is made up of respectable families. Thus, the underclass – people who are unemployed and perhaps engaged in criminal activity, who neither live in stable families nor aspire to steady jobs – were seen as politically unreliable for socialist purposes. Given that context, Foucault's sustained critique of the specifically moral foundations of bourgeois society put him rather on the margins of all the various Marxisms of the day.

Influenced by the spirit of 1968, by Bataille's work on transgression and by Nietzsche's critique of Judeo-Christian morality (and possibly also by his own experience as a gay man growing up in the homophobic society of the 1940s and 1950s), Foucault parted company with the respectable-family ethos that the communist movement since Marx had taken for granted. In these lectures, he reflects in a strikingly non-Marxist and non-moralistic manner on the tendency of large parts of the nineteenth-century working classes to spend their wages right away, to get drunk, to take Monday off work and so on. Refusals of the capitalist work ethic amongst the early industrial working classes, especially well documented for France by social historians of the 1970s, are discussed by Foucault under the awkwardly worded banner of 'illegalisms of dissipation' (Foucault 2015: 188–92). 'Dissipation' (a term connoting spendthrift habits and short-term pleasure-seeking) is here treated not as a vice sapping the moral fabric of the working class, as the Communist Party would have seen it, but rather as a form of resistance to the discipline of early industrial capitalism. Foucault does not quite say that in the 'civil war' that was early industrial capitalism, seeking dissipation and rejecting the work ethic was a weapon wielded against capitalists by workers who were toiling away in unregulated, unsafe factories; but that would be a logical corollary of the comments about civil war as the normal state of society discussed above.

The importance given to the term 'illegalisms of dissipation' (which is not discussed in *Discipline and Punish*) shows that Foucault used social historians' work on the early industrial working class to start opening a path towards post-Marxist and anti-moralistic critiques of capitalism. The illegalisms of dissipation are explained by being contrasted to the 'illegalisms of depredation'. What were the illegalisms of depredation? Foucault tells us that in the early days of capitalism, bourgeois writers denounced those who hunted game illegally in newly enclosed and/or privatized commons and forests. Bourgeois writers also condemned as thieves those who continued to benefit from traditional forms of income supplementation, such as the London dockworkers' customary entitlement to collecting the sugar, coffee and grain spilled while loading and unloading ships. These forms of economic resistance to capitalist wage labour – often based on older notions of 'the moral economy' – are called, in these lectures, 'illegalisms of depredation'. Now, the history of property-related illegalisms was the bread and butter of the Marxist historians of Foucault's time (and was also important for the great Marxist theorist Louis Althusser, who had little interest in history but apparently always made his students – including Foucault himself – read Marx's articles on German peasants' theft of wood from forests in the 1840s).

By contrast, the illegalism of dissipation – which does not directly challenge property but rather challenges the ideal of the morally upright, sober, family-based working class – was not treated seriously or positively by mainstream Marxism. So Foucault asks: if historians have shown that significant numbers of working men refused to marry and spent much of their pay on reckless Saturday night pleasures, how should this refusal of conventional morality be regarded? Foucault argues, against economistic forms of Marxism, that the 'illegalism of dissipation is more dangerous than [that of] depredation' (Foucault 2015: 190). Why? Because while the customary entitlements to goods or opportunities that capitalism turns into 'theft' remain largely individual, there is a collective revolutionary potential in activities such as celebrating 'Saint Monday' (a nineteenth-century French working-class tradition not specifically named by Foucault). In Foucault's eyes, the collective refusal of moral regulation 'confront[s] bourgeois wealth with more serious dangers' (ibid.: 191) than better-known property illegalisms such as poaching game.[2]

I am not sure whether social historians would agree with Foucault that the refusal of moral norms threatened the early bourgeois order more than breaching property laws by helping oneself to game or to some of the master's property. But whether historically accurate or not, these lectures present the emerging bourgeois order of early industrial capitalism as more vulnerable to moral challenges than to economic challenges – very much against the grain of all the Marxisms of the day.

And there is an interesting link here to the rise of criminological sciences. Foucault proceeds to tell his audience that the Herculean ruling-class effort that had to be made in order to 'moralize' and discipline workers and prevent the eruption of a counter-morality amongst the working classes owed a great deal not only to Christian leaders but also to criminology. By 'criminology' Foucault primarily means not academic criminology, which did not yet exist during the relevant time, but rather the work of punishment reformers, prison doctors and prison administration experts.

The role of criminal law reform and criminology in securing the bourgeois social–moral order

In order to explain Foucault's account of penal reformers' moralizing role – that is, of the role of proto-criminology in the securing of the bourgeois order in the nineteenth century – we need to return to a point, made halfway through the lectures, that sheds new light on Foucault's view of the Enlightenment reform of criminal justice. Cesare Beccaria and his late eighteenth-century reformer contemporaries, Foucault explains, courageously attempted, for the first time in the Christian world, to separate religion and law. Beccaria is justly famous in criminological and in legal circles because he attempted to construct a rational criminal justice system that would eliminate cruelty and would operate on the assumption that people should be considered as rational in the economic sense of the word. Beccaria (and, in Britain, Jeremy Bentham as well) marks a radical break from the ancient moralization of offending and deviance that in the common-law world is perhaps best embodied in the writings of William Blackstone on criminal law. Foucault states (quite uncontroversially) that with the rise of rationalism and utilitarianism along Beccaria lines, 'there is a break between moral wrongdoing and infraction' (Foucault 2015: 107). This separation of morality and law was in keeping with the rationalistic side of the Enlightenment. But, as the previous discussion of the illegalisms of dissipation makes clear, a real danger for bourgeois society emerges if it turns out that people, in significant numbers, refuse to behave as economically rational subjects – as was the case with workers engaged in dissipation, who got drunk and failed to show up for work on Monday morning.

According to Foucault, what happened, given working-class resistance to adopting the capitalist work ethic, is that Beccaria's pure form of rationalism became sidelined as the nineteenth century wore on. Rationalism was supplanted by moralisms of different kinds (Catholic as well as Quaker or mainstream Protestant, we could add; though Foucault does not deal with religious differences here). In Britain, Patrick Colquhoun devised an intricate system of hybrid economic-moral 'police' – meaning municipal and administrative regulations – that would supplement the criminal law through local regulations that assumed that workers would indeed engage in dissipation whenever possible, measures that departed significantly from the rational-choice model of human behaviour favoured by Beccaria (Foucault 2015:

108). And in Britain too, one sees the overtly religious Quakers take pride of place in the reform of criminal justice. It is in keeping with the more explicit focus on moral regulation in the lectures series that the Quakers play a far more prominent role in the elaboration of the penitentiary system in these lectures than is the case in *Discipline and Punish*.

In a passage that was similarly not included in *Discipline and Punish*, Foucault goes on to argue that criminology's importance for the formation of bourgeois society (with 'criminology' again meaning, primarily, nineteenth-century reformers) is precisely that the science of punishment did not in fact follow Beccaria's model, but rather returned, early in the nineteenth century, to a more or less Christian view of the importance of instilling good habits. This argument about the importance of moral regulation as a motor force of criminal justice – which goes in and out of view as the lectures progress – is perhaps most clearly laid out in the March 7 lecture. The offender, Foucault noted, might be considered a rational citizen at trial; but once declared guilty, the offender becomes a criminal soul/body, a deviant in need of moral reform. Thus, criminology – that is, 'a kind of research claiming to correct, to regenerate the individual' (Foucault 2015: 177) – emerges to take over the post-verdict space; and its emergence allows criminal law theorists to continue focusing on rationality along Kantian or Beccarian lines (to this day). This is 'the essential duality of the [modern] penal system' (ibid.).

Criminology, therefore (meaning administrative knowledge of criminality and rehabilitation) is thus the essential supplement to modern, rational-choice, humane criminal law. The process by which guilt is determined may be run on a Beccaria-style rational-choice basis, in the best of courts; but those who are found guilty are immediately turned over to a system that consistently and overtly uses old-fashioned moralization.

Beyond Marxism – and beyond systematicity

Readers today may need to be reminded that all forms of Marxism look at criminal justice and punishment from the point of view of class relations, and pay little attention to such empirical details as the particular form that punishment takes at a certain place and time – although the signal work by Rusche and Kirchheimer (1939) on punishment did pay some attention to specific practices. Foucault was never a real Marxist, of course. But it is interesting that in these lectures Foucault, while speaking in a more Marxist language than in his published books and in subsequent sets of lectures, perhaps to better connect with his audience, nevertheless makes a move that would enable future left-wing criminologists to analyse various forms of punishment from a post-Marxist point of view. Foucault's ideas paved the way for contemporary criminologists today investigating how different penal strategies, instead of being understood as reflecting changes in the ruling class's composition or priorities, in line with Marxist class determinism, can be understood as creating particular subjectivities, souls and spatiotemporalities that are certainly connected to economic relations but are not fully explained by these relations. It is difficult for younger readers today, in a world in which there are a multiplicity of progressive perspectives, to appreciate the creativity and courage required in 1973 to lay the basis for a post-Marxist framework that would remain resolutely on the left and anti-capitalist, but would shed the ontologies and epistemologies of Marxism's many versions.

As he wrote and delivered these lectures, Foucault came to the view that power is best seen not as possessed by a dominant class or even a ruling bloc, but rather as fluid and ever-present (including amongst dominated groups), and perhaps also as plural (though the heterogeneity of forms of power/knowledge is not yet very visible in these lectures). The view that power is everywhere and is always fluid and changing is clearly adapted from Nietzsche, though (fortunately) shorn of Nietzsche's questionable vitalist philosophy. Later, Foucault would push this analysis beyond Nietzsche: he would reject the idea that one can speak about 'power' in general, and would emphasize the differences between various power processes (e.g. biopolitics, pastoral power, governmentality). But the heterogeneity of power only becomes a key theme in later years.

In that context, one important feature of *Discipline and Punish* that is lacking in these lectures is precisely the sharp contrast drawn in the book between juridical or sovereign exercises of power on the one hand, and discipline on the other. Juridical/sovereign power is mentioned in these lectures, but is not at the centre. In the book, by focusing on the dyad of juridical versus disciplinary power, Foucault does begin to go beyond Nietzsche's unitary concept of power; but, as he moves toward isolating 'discipline' and differentiating it from 'sovereignty', he also removes from view many interesting ideas presented in the lectures (such as the notion of civil war as the default setting for social relations, or the complex historical analysis of working-class illegalisms). Therefore, those who want to gain a deeper understanding of the twists and turns of Foucault's complex and unsystematic work would do well to do close readings of these lectures, and compare and contrast them with different texts (and not only *Discipline and Punish*). Different texts on similar topics do overlap, of course; but the apparent inconsistencies caused by the constant effort to rewrite and revise and change terminology provide us today not only with substantive insights but also, more importantly, with a model of how to keep thinking instead of merely repeating or refining what we have thought in the past.

Like most intellectuals, Foucault tended to overemphasize his own intellectual consistency, especially in interviews, where he often said disingenuous things along the lines of 'My work has always been focused on (subjectivity, power, etc.)'. But in these lectures we can see for ourselves that the ideas presented in *Discipline and Punish*, which have now become mainstays of critical criminology, represent but a partial, simplified version of a complex body of work on the history and theory of punishment that is less elegant and systematic but more wide-ranging, dynamic and, in my view, far more fruitful for us today than we have previously thought.

Notes

1 Foucault's 'Preface to Transgression' was originally published just after Bataille's death, in 1963, and it is translated with some slight changes as 'A Preface to Transgression' in Foucault (1998: 69–87). Footnotes 7 and 8 on p. 17 of the volume under review provide a

thorough and erudite account of Foucault's writings on transgression and their context.

2 The discussions of both illegalisms of property depredation and illegalisms of moral dissipation are very male-centred, in keeping with the historical sources on working-class history on which Foucault relied. It is worth noting that at the time, before the flourishing of feminist perspectives in working-class history, male workers' drinking habits could be reclassified by someone like Foucault as a form of resistance, whereas nobody was then attempting to reclaim or validate women workers' 'vices'. The moralism that is present in such classic Marxist sources on early industrial life as Friedrich Engels' *The Condition of the Working-Class in England in 1844* (1936) was challenged by Foucault only in regard to male workers.

Bibliography

Engels, Friedrich. 1936. *The Condition of the Working-Class in England in 1844*. Translated by Florence Kelley Wischnewetzky. London: Allen.

Foucault, Michel. 1977. *Discipline and Punish: The Birth of the Prison*. Translated by Alan Sheridan. New York: Vintage.

Foucault, Michel. 1998. *Aesthetics, Method, and Epistemology: Essential Works of Foucault, 1954–1984, Vol. 2*. Edited by James D. Faubion. New York: New Press.

Foucault, Michel. 2015. *The Punitive Society: Lectures at the Collège de France 1972–1973*. Edited by Bernard E. Harcourt. Translated by Graham Burchell. Basingstoke: Palgrave Macmillan.

O'Malley, Pat. 2009. *The Currency of Justice: Fines and Damages in Consumer Society*. London: Routledge.

Rusche, Georg and Otto Kirchheimer. 1939. *Punishment and Social Structure*. New York: Columbia University Press.

Chapter 7

The forensic roots of modern science and law

The publication of a previously unknown set of lectures entitled *Wrong-Doing, Truth-Telling: The Function of Avowal in Justice* (Foucault 2014), delivered by Foucault in 1981 at the University of Louvain's eminent criminology institute, has shed important new light on the incredible richness of Foucault's contributions to both sociolegal and criminological research. The bare fact that, when already very famous, Foucault agreed to prepare seven major lectures and lead a six-week seminar series specifically for criminal law and criminology scholars is in itself a sign that he was less dismissive of criminological research than has generally been thought. The series of lectures arose from an invitation by Françoise Tulkens, a noted criminal law professor at Louvain who later became vice-president of the European Court of Human Rights. The 1973 Collège de France 'Punitive society' lectures discussed in the previous chapter also constitute an important contribution to criminology, of course; but a good deal of the material in those lectures was reworked for inclusion in *Discipline and Punish* (Foucault 1977). In addition, while the texts of the different Collège de France lecture series remained unavailable for many years after Foucault's death in 1984, the existence of those series of lectures (most of which were made available to zealous researchers in the form of audiotapes that could be consulted in an archive in Paris) was well known in the scholarly world. By contrast, many reasonably well-informed criminologists working with Foucault's texts did not even know that the Louvain lectures existed until they were edited and published (in French and English in 2012 and 2014 respectively) by American criminologist Bernard Harcourt and Louvain's Fabienne Brion. And neither did many of us English-speaking scholars know that the related Brazil lectures published under the title 'Truth and Juridical Forms' even existed until they were included, very belatedly, in volume 3 of the *The Essential Works of Michel Foucault* (Foucault 2000: 1–89).

In this chapter I will go back and forth between the lectures given in Rio de Janeiro in 1973 ('Truth and Juridical Forms') and those given in Louvain in 1981. Going back and forth between the texts may perhaps be a little confusing for the reader, but is necessary given the considerable overlap between these two sources. The reading of the two sets of lectures will develop my argument that, if one reads these talks together, one can conclude that in them Foucault used the opportunities provided by lecture invitations outside France to develop an important, if not exhaustive, account of the forensic roots of modern law and science, an account that sheds a very new light on the issue of what Foucault's work can do for legal studies and criminology.

As shown earlier in the book, especially in Chapter 6, Foucault's work on the genealogy of the state and of modern political theory carefully developed in the Collège de France lectures entitled *Society Must be Defended* (Foucault 2003) – but also found in bits and pieces throughout the scattered work on governmentality, security and police (Foucault 2007) – is also highly relevant to criminology and criminal justice scholar today. Without a broader understanding of major historical shifts in what state power is and how it is exercised one cannot hope to really appreciate the importance of the choices historical actors (such as state officials) made in using one rather than another mechanism to govern crime or criminals at any particular point. Using Foucault's innovative genealogy of modern states to put criminal justice in a larger context is certainly necessary and worthwhile. However, over the next few years – as the lectures given outside Paris, and especially in Louvain, are digested by scholars – it may be that a consensus emerges that the most important set of Foucaultian resources that directly and explicitly bear on criminal justice and criminal law is to be found in the Rio and the

Louvain lectures. In these talks Foucault presented an extremely original historical analysis of a variety of techniques devised, mainly in legal or quasi-legal contexts, to uncover and establish not so much factual scientific truths as what I would call 'truths that really matter' – truths about crimes that are also truths about personal identity and ethical responsibility.

The truth about who committed a heinous deed; about whether she or he is morally responsible; about whether the act was an uncharacteristic outburst or a symptom of an underlying deep identity; and what the individual story says about the larger social relations are questions that are fodder for tabloids and may be of no significance to highbrow science. However, I would argue that there are reasons these questions continue to be explored in contemporary fiction and drama as well as in journalism and popular books (although Foucault does not explicitly discuss or even mention contemporary genres, especially lowbrow ones that show the continuing relevance of the forms of truth-seeking first developed for non-legal purposes in Greek tragedies).

Briefly mentioning contemporary cultural products that ask the same questions about crime, truth and the criminal's identity as ancient Greek plays can help make Foucault's erudite excursions into often obscure sources more relevant to today. Despite the current prestige of cold, impersonal knowledge formats such as data-driven risk assessments, in everyday life the search for truth is generally not impersonal and numerical but rather embodied, personalized and dramatic. Today's generation can thus learn a great deal that applies to our own culture from Foucault's exploration of the profound but historically shifting connections between what he calls 'avowal' on the one hand, and the pursuit of justice on the other – the connections at the centre of the Louvain lectures collected in *Wrong-Doing, Truth-Telling*. And, fortunately for criminology, the evolving connections between personal truths and state justice were developed for both Louvain and Rio audiences through detailed analyses of developments in criminal procedure – not a subject area that otherwise features, in a sustained manner, in any of the works Foucault published in his lifetime.

The sketch of the history of 'truth-telling' contained in the two series of lectures shows that, in Foucault's view, criminal procedure (including the proto-criminal procedure arrangements of premodern times) was the site on which key scientific knowledge procedures were pioneered. The fact that Foucault was not interested in criminal law or criminal procedure for its own sake, but rather studied them only insofar as the justice system served as a site on which techniques of truth-telling and truth-certification were developed that would then be exported to other fields, has a great deal of potential to show today's experts on the history of criminal procedure that their subject area is not as self-contained as is generally thought. As will be shown in more detail below, the 'avowal' of the subtitle of the Louvain lectures (*aveu* in French)[1] is shown to be an important and flexible technique that developed through various attempts to determine truth in the context of justice, whether legal justice or the kind of justice sought by the protagonists of classical Greek tragedies. Avowing what one has done – and also what one is, as in the case of 'deviant' identities – is a knowledge move that, as mentioned above, is extremely important in contemporary popular culture (especially crime- and police-centred genres) as well as in contemporary legal proceedings and crime reporting. Therefore, the genealogy of avowal carried out here has many possible applications and implications. While focusing mainly on practices of avowal, the Louvain lectures also present Foucault's research on the historical antecedents of a host of other more or less legal knowledge practices – from oath-taking to the emergence of formal adjudication – that also have implications for how we think of the relationship between criminal law history and the history of powers/knowledges more generally. And it is to this latter theme (the rise of formal procedures in criminal justice) that the Rio lectures contribute significantly. If the first major theme of this chapter is avowal, the second is 'inquiry'.

In both sets of lectures Foucault argues that it was in proto-legal or quasi-legal contexts associated with personal avowal that the modern notion of an inquiry developed. The inquiry, in general, is a distinctly modern approach to truth-seeking. The word 'inquiry' is not as likely to be used today in scholarly or philosophical contexts as it was 300 years ago; but governments today routinely organize 'inquiries' to sort out policy problems or (very relevant to the Louvain lectures) to uncover the unpleasant, hidden truth about events, especially scandalous events. Official inquiries are often given legal mandates that prevent them from formally assigning legal responsibility to any one individual; but nevertheless assigning responsibility (often to government institutions or whole governments) is in fact the whole point of the inquiry. In today's inquiries, as in the proto-inquiries Foucault dredges up from obscure corners of European cultural and legal history, the search for true facts is inextricable from the search for moral truth and the consequent assignation of responsibility. The fact that formal apologies often follow from inquiries is one sign that avowal is alive and well today (even if many publicly broadcast avowals by people in high places are today likely to be concocted by public relations firms).

A second important point – important more for legal scholars or law students, perhaps, than for the public at large – is the fact that the inquiry, as a distinct knowledge form not present in the ancient world, was developed in innovations in legal procedure. This revelation turns on its head the conventional view that for Foucault law in general is derivative or unimportant and has been replaced by discipline and governmentality.

The place of the Louvain and Rio lectures in Foucault's work

Before delving into the content of the lectures more deeply, it is appropriate to briefly consider why Foucault's important research on proto-judicial practices of inquiry and truth-telling remained on the back burner rather than being worked up into books. My explanation, which is necessarily speculative, is as follows. The last two books published in Foucault's lifetime, volumes 2 and 3 of the *History of Sexuality* (published in French in 1983 and 1984 and in English in 1984 and 1988), were concerned with questions of ethics, especially those covered by Foucault's term 'the care of self'. The care of self is for Foucault no hedonistic self-improvement project. The term refers to the lifelong, conscious cultivation of practices for governing oneself in an enlightened manner in everyday life,[2] through careful reflection on such mundane choices as the meals we have, the friends we seek, how we talk with our friends, and how we manage our sexual desires. The care of self is not a distinct sphere of life, but rather a particular dimension of all aspects of one's life. Thus, care of self could under some circumstances include something as apparently trivial as getting a pedicure, but only if this is part of a larger conscious project to work on one's freedom. A person who was born male and is in the process of transitioning to female, for example, might carefully explore and then purchase a range of everyday commodified practices that are gender-affirming, including a pedicure and a new hairstyle. But neither nail salons nor hair salons are necessarily sites for consciously working towards one's chosen 'self'. So what is and is not a care of self practice depends very much on the biographical and social contexts.

The reflective care of self, both in ancient Greek thought and for Foucault, is closely connected to, is indeed a condition for, the wise governance of others. Drawing from ancient Greek sources, Foucault suggested many times that, even today, those who seek leadership positions need to engage in self-reflection and wise self-governance. However, in the *History of Sexuality* volumes the political dimensions of the care of self remain muted. It could be said that, just as *Discipline and Punish* gave the reading public a clearer, more coherent but also simpler picture of the rise of modern disciplinary methods than what was found in the less tightly written, more open-ended texts of the *Punitive Society* lectures (2015, discussed in Chapter 6), so too the last two books published during Foucault's lifetime (volumes 2 and 3 of *The History of Sexuality*) were presented primarily as contributions to ethics. The broader political focus of volume 1 – which, as mentioned in Chapter 3, contains among other highly political passages the famous discussion of 'biopolitics' – was in the subsequent volumes relegated to the background, probably for the sake of consistency and readability. Given the focus on ethical self-development of these last two published books (with that narrower focus being also visible in some of the lectures he gave late in life, notably at Berkeley in 2001), it made sense for Foucault to leave the realm of law and politics to one side.

Thus, the Louvain and the Rio lectures presented research that was carefully left out of both *Discipline and Punish* and the last two volumes of *History of Sexuality*. But now it is possible for us to read, together, lectures that were given to audiences in very different locations, eight years apart. With the advantage of hindsight, we can see that Foucault's research on the history of practices used to establish the facts of crimes and incite wrong-doers to avow their crime (or, later, their 'bad' self) could easily have become a major book unto itself. The proto-book to which I refer consists of the three lectures given in Rio in 1973 (Foucault 2000); the seven lectures given in Louvain in 1981; and three interviews, mainly concerned with legal and political subjects, given by Foucault while visiting Louvain and included in the volume *Wrong-Doing Truth-Telling* (2014).

What Foucault did not clearly state in writings published in his lifetime – but which has become clear since then and is very important for sociolegal and criminological scholarship – is that legal institutions, like most other institutions, are not hard-wired to any one governing logic or any one type of power. It is thus not appropriate to make generalizations about whether 'law' in general is sovereign, disciplinary, governmental or anything else. Even criminal law and criminal justice are not domains of pure 'sovereignty'/coercive law. While in other work Foucault explored forms of power/knowledge that are not disciplinary and are sometimes found in criminal justice contexts (e.g. pastoral power), these lectures emphasize the unpredictable appropriation of various truth techniques in all manner of new contexts, without using any epochal or quasi-epochal generalizations. The quasi-epochal contrast set out in *Discipline and Punish* between old and new, between sovereign power and disciplinary power, was tremendously influential precisely because it was a sharp analytical dividing line – rather than a full and nuanced historical account.

In the Louvain lectures Foucault makes a number of fairly well-informed comments about legal and judicial procedures in ancient Greece and in medieval Europe; but the lectures do not amount either to a full history or – more importantly for most readers – to a theory of law or a theory of justice. Contrary to the impression about the decline of law created by *Discipline and Punish*, Foucault here shows that modern scientific and psychiatric truth-seeking borrowed, consciously or not, a number of key techniques from legal and quasi-legal projects and institutions, including the interrogation of witnesses and the inciting of suspects to confess their crime and/or their evil disposition. The pressure put on people to acknowledge or avow one's crime, one's madness, one's deviant desires, etc. is a widely distributed phenomenon, one that allows Foucault to bring together his interest in the history of truth and his equally strong interest in the history of 'subjectification' – although the implications for analysing current-day practices, from forensic investigation to confession-centred reality-TV shows, are not developed by Foucault himself. But there are indications that in the last two or three years of his life Foucault seemed anxious to bring together these different research agendas, as he explained in the first of the 1983 set of lectures at the Collège de France (Foucault 2010: 4–7). Further, the fact that, in front of Louvain's audience of law professors and criminologists, Foucault argued that judicial or quasi-judicial efforts to uncover, certify and assign responsibility for misdeeds gave rise, unwittingly, to innovations in knowledge-gathering that made the scientific revolution and modern philosophy possible is a surprising claim that, however much it becomes qualified – as it no doubt will – by historians, should profoundly transform sociolegal scholars' appreciation of Foucault's work.

Having given a sense of the context and the importance of the lectures on legal and other practices of truth-telling, it is now time to consider some of the key themes developed in them, giving central place to the Louvain lectures but also including the Rio lectures (which overlap in a few places) in the discussion.

Practices of veridiction and practices of jurisdiction in 'pre-law' Greece

Working on a genealogy of avowal did more than allow Foucault to speak directly to a legal and criminological audience familiar with techniques of legal truth-seeking. It also allowed him to finally bring his interest in the government of the self and the government of others together with his Nietzsche-inspired work on the history of practices of truth. The site upon which this coming together of what might otherwise seem separate research interests (the ethical, the political, the epistemological) was a partial history of what he called 'veridiction', a neologism devised by Foucault in the inaugural Louvain lecture, in a deliberate parallel with 'jurisdiction'.

Oedipus' quest for truth about a crime, a quest which famously reveals that he is the very criminal he is pursuing, is the most important chapter in the history of veridiction, and thus in Foucault's genealogy of avowal. But in both the Rio lectures (Foucault 2000) and in the Louvain lectures (2014), the analysis of the complex relationships between truth, justice and personal identity found in Sophocles' Oedipus story is preceded by a close reading of an older text: a passage from Homer featuring a chariot race organized by Achilles to honour the memory of his slain comrade Patroclus.

The chariot race, or rather the Homeric description of the long discussion that followed the race, would not seem relevant to the history of modern justice since it was not framed as part of any legal proceeding or quasi-criminal investigation. But Foucault adopted the classical scholar Louis Gernet's claim that the description of the chariot race is an example of 'pre-law' (Foucault 2014: 30), specifically a predecessor of later formal adjudication. The post-race debate does not focus on who won – an uninteresting question to the participants since the goddess Athena intervened to make her favourite come first. It focuses only on who deserves second versus third prize. And the proto-inquiry into who is the rightful silver medal winner reveals and affirms a deeper truth (ibid.: 40–42). Why? In the masculine Greek warrior context, the truth that mattered was that of the relative worth and honour of the participants, a truth not always matched by clock-time results. What happened is that, after Athena had divinely intervened to have her favourite win, the real fight became the one for second prize, and the apparently stronger and better contender had his chariot blocked in a sharp turn by a 'lesser' contender. The warrior who came in second – and could claim to be the real winner if one discounts divine intervention – eventually recognizes that his opponent was in fact stronger/worthier. He acknowledges that he should just get the third prize, not the second, despite having in fact come in second.

Foucault highlights the fact that the contenders, being part of a society of equal honour-seeking warriors, mediate their own dispute. There is no judge. There is also no prosecutor and no jury. But, perhaps more surprisingly, people who witnessed the events are not called upon as witnesses. Achilles, as the race organizer, hands out the prizes but does not act as judge; and, more significantly, the race official known in Greek as the *histor*, who acts as a kind of line judge, is not called as a quasi-legal witness. As Foucault says in the Rio lectures: 'Curiously, in this text by Homer the parties involved do not call upon the person who saw, the famous witness' (Foucault 2000: 18).

In pre-law Greece, then, the game of truth (which is also a game of justice) that is at work is a strictly aristocratic one in which honourable warriors settle their own disputes. Foucault tells his audience that the absence of markers of 'real' law (judges, witnesses, etc.) might make some think that the chariot race, like other pre-legal disputes, has no relevance to the history of adjudication and formal law. But he then sides with those sociolegal scholars who see a direct continuity between the older, agonistic practices for determining the just outcome of a horizontal struggle on the one hand, and formal practices of adjudication on the other. This analysis echoes much of the sociolegal literature on dispute resolution in both Western and non-Western societies, since both historians and anthropologists have emphasized that self-mediation or contests to see which party can gather the most support are the direct ancestors of formal legal processes including formal adjudication.

Incidentally, when English translations use the word 'judicial' to translate Foucault's *judiciaire*, as is the case in the lectures being discussed, a reader who is only familiar with common law systems may gain the wrong impression. In many civil law systems, including France, some judges investigate complaints, even occasionally attending scenes of crime; and in many countries specialized bodies of police officers work under the direction of a judge to investigate matters ('judicial police'). The fact that investigation – finding out 'who done it' – and adjudication are not nearly as separate in civil law systems as they are in common law jurisdictions means that Foucault's account of 'judicial' truth-seeking is relevant for legal and policing history generally; the term *judiciaire* is not exclusively attached to courtroom settings or verdict rendering.

A related point that underlines that the risks of translation are multiplied when one is translating not only from one language to another but from one legal system to another concerns the related word 'juridical', as used for example by Paul Rabinow and James Faubion in their edition of the Rio lectures, which they entitled 'Truth and *Juridical* Forms' (Foucault 2000). In English, 'juridical' is not a word in common use, having somewhat philosophical, jurisprudential connotations; in French, by contrast (and in other Romance languages as well), 'juridical' is an everyday word covering any process or any authority in the legal system. (The French word *légale* simply means 'in conformity with current law', that is, legal in the sense of the opposite of illegal.) I would argue that the Rio lectures should have been entitled 'Truth and *Legal* Forms' – since they are mainly concerned with procedure, not with anything resembling jurisprudence or legal theory. The term 'legal forms' would resonate better with existing sociolegal scholarship, and would not sound as technical as 'juridical'.

The issue of how to translate and interpret the key words *judiciaire* and *juridique* is of more than trivial interest. Foucault's quest to establish hitherto invisible continuities among a number of diverse types of dispute and types of justice-seeking process (some lying well outside any legal system) is easier to grasp if we make less use of technical terms with a narrow institutional meaning, such as 'judicial' and 'juridical', and more use of terms that – thanks to the work of law and society scholars – now have a very broad, cross-institutional meaning, such as 'legal'.

Be that as it may, if Homer's or rather Achilles' chariot race represents a dispute resolution mechanism that is oriented to revealing and confirming established gradations of honour and worth among warriors – without any need for an external judge or even impartial factual witnesses, since the truth of 'who done it' is not what is being sought – Homer nevertheless does mention a mechanism that persists into the present, namely, the use of a solemn oath. Foucault then recounts how the oath evolves in works by Hesiod, stating that the oath gradually turns into an act by which a new figure – the external, formal judge – is called into what had previously been a 'private' dispute (Foucault 2014: 45–50).

I have no idea whether Foucault is correct in claiming that (in Hesiod) it is the oaths taken by the parties that authorize someone to act as judge, rather than, as is the case today, the oath being a mechanism by which the judge who administers it binds the parties to the process. But the witness's oath is one of the many taken-for-granted legal techniques of truth that would certainly benefit from both historical and sociological investigation. In my view, taking the oath seriously rather than (as is usually done) blackboxing it can help us understand that, in general, knowledge processes can feature a separation of techniques for *establishing truth* – such as cross-examining witnesses or following the scientific method in the laboratory – from techniques for *certifying or guaranteeing truths after they have been established*. The oath is a technique to certify or guarantee a truth presented by someone else, just as peer review is a technique for certifying previously established scientific truths. The oath, however, certifies truth claims beforehand, just before they are spoken, whereas peer review does so afterwards.

The third Louvain lecture, given on April 28, 1981 (Foucault 2014), overlaps quite a bit with the second of the earlier Rio lectures. In Rio, Foucault acknowledged that his reading of Oedipus' truth-seeking is in part a response or a turning upside down of the then-established readings of this figure. Ever since Freud's work became popular, educated Westerners have used the word 'Oedipal' to signal the unconscious as such. Without drawing attention to his own clever inversion, Foucault shows that Oedipus' terrible fate can be read not as the result of keeping unconscious desires 'in the dark' and out of sight, but rather as the unintended effect of too much interest in the truth. The Oedipal 'complex' Foucault uncovers is nothing less than the inextricable link between power and knowledge, he claims (Foucault 2000: 17).

In Louvain, by contrast, Foucault forgets psychoanalysis – having dispatched it in *The History of Sexuality Volume I* just a couple of years earlier (Foucault 1976) – and instead opens the lecture on Oedipus with a sociolegal reflection on the extent to which the history of European theatre (in which Greek tragedies are of course a key chapter) can be read as a history of 'the representation of law' (Foucault 2014: 59). And, he adds in an aside, it is not only the grand classic French theatre of Corneille that can be read as a representation of law; popular culture too (he offhandedly mentions the American western) is centrally concerned with 'the confrontation of rights, the confrontation of law and vengeance, the right of conquest' (ibid.).

Still in Louvain, but reiterating some of what he had said years earlier in Brazil, Foucault then goes on to explain that in classical Greece many of the truths that mattered were uttered either by kings who could, Leviathan-like, declare that their word was both just and true, or else by supernatural oracles. Sophocles' tragedy *Oedipus Rex*, according to Foucault, departs from these conventions and experiments with new procedures for establishing truth for purposes of justice, procedures that in somewhat different form are still current today. The oracle is initially consulted when a plague afflicts the city of Thebes; but the prophetic words of the oracle do not have any effect until Oedipus – who is simultaneously the detective, the suspect, the judge and the quasi-executioner (since at the end he puts out his own eyes) – starts a quest that features several key legal actors and procedures. The oracle is thus not the real source or the guarantor of truth as it might have been in earlier times: it is only a device to set Oedipus in motion. The realm of the supernatural has not been eliminated – God is not yet dead; but truth, in this play, is most definitely discovered and then certified by humans.

If the oath is one legal technique whose origins and importance are highlighted by Foucault, the second proto-modern legal truth technique analysed here is that of witnessing. The truth about Oedipus' real parentage, while hinted at by the oracle, is revealed neither by prophecy nor by kingly decree (the older sources of truth), but rather by the testimony of a low-status character, a shepherd, who is probably a slave. This highlights the new role of witnesses and the associated form of truth that came to be called 'evidence' – new, that is, in relation to the Homeric dispute about the chariot race, a dispute which, as mentioned above, did not prompt witnesses to be called. As the Rio lectures put it:

> we can say that the entire Oedipus play is a way of shifting the enunciation of truth from a prophetic and prescriptive type of discourse to a retrospective one that is no longer characterized by prophecy but, rather, by evidence.
>
> (Foucault 2000: 23; see Louvain lecture of April 28, Foucault 2014)

In addition to witnesses and evidence, the third element of European modern justice is the jury. And Foucault notes that the evidence produced by witnesses is subject to being weighed and certified, in Sophocles' play, by a body that functions like a modern jury or a 'tribunal' ('court' would be a better translation here, in my view) – namely, the chorus. Giving numerous examples of the way in which the chorus appears to validate what Oedipus is slowly discovering, Foucault concludes that 'the chorus is the body that tests, accepts, or refuses [evidence], and establishes the truth told' (2014: 67).[3]

And now we come to the 'avowal' of the Louvain lecture series subtitle. The fourth proto-legal truth-seeking technique that Foucault uncovers, the avowal, is the crucial link that connects a practice of self (whether the confession of a wrong committed or the acknowledgement of an inner deviant identity) to the machinery of justice. The process through which the chorus comes to understand and acknowledge the truths that matter – that Oedipus unwittingly murdered his father and equally unwittingly married his mother – is thus reiterated and paralleled in the play by Oedipus' avowal. There is an evolving 'correlation between Oedipus' recognition of who he is and what he has done and the chorus's recognition of the juridical validity of the truth' (Foucault 2014: 67). It would not have worked for Sophocles to send a fictional proto-detective to find out who killed Laius – such a move might have created a good Sherlock Holmes story but not a memorable tragedy. To be a memorable tragic figure rather than just someone who mistakenly committed two major crimes, Oedipus has to be somehow brought around, by his own discoveries, to the point of avowing that he is the worst of all possible criminals. That is far more dramatic than the usual police procedural.

The comment on Oedipus' avowal is a crucial passage in the lectures. The inaugural lecture of the Louvain series opened with a scene not from a legal but from a medical text featuring a nineteenth-century asylum doctor forcing a patient called Leuret to 'confess' to being mad. The patient first insists that he is in fact being pursued by invisible beings; but, after being subjected to a series of sudden cold showers, he acknowledges that perhaps he is indeed mad and it is all in his imagination. Foucault's interest here is in showing that even when a confession – in this case, about having a mental illness – has to be coerced, and lacks the indicia of sincerity, authorities do not want to proceed without that acknowledgement, that avowal. What Foucault is showing here, in an understated manner, is that purely objective truth (Oedipus killed Laius, Monsieur Leuret is insane) is inadequate because it fails to bind the patient's/offender's subjectivity to the truth. And the binding of practices of subjectivity to practices of truth cannot happen in private; it has to be made public. In other words, it has to be certified (certification or guaranteeing being my own terms, not Foucault's, incidentally). The truth admitted by the subject – the avowal – has to be subsequently certified by colleagues, family members and legal authorities, in the case of the mentally ill, or by the courts and by the media and the public, in the case of offenders.

Foucault does not explicitly say that legal venues and legal proceedings were the sites in which techniques later used in medical and scientific practices of verification, such as second opinions and presenting work at conferences, were first invented. But it is clear Foucault believed, and showed, that the study of the history of legal procedures is of importance far beyond legal studies, since so many legal and quasi-legal evidentiary inventions dating back to ancient Greece were later borrowed for other uses, including all manner of modern scientific endeavours. Peer review, for example, could be seen as a modern-day, scholarly descendant of Sophocles' chorus – although to the victims of unfair anonymous reviews, peer review might seem more like the oracular irrational pronouncement that Max Weber (1968) saw in the English jury.

The practices of avowal and other forms of truth-telling whose prehistory Foucault traces were later adopted in a variety of settings. From a criminological perspective it is clear that such practices can be found within what by the early twentieth century came to be the special domain of detectives, that is, criminal investigation. Oedipus famously does recognize and avow his crimes, and indeed goes on to punish himself – though only after the truth has been formally narrated by witnesses and recognized by the jury/chorus. But, in addition, Oedipus also plays, simultaneously, the role of detective ('detective' is my own word here, not Foucault's). In other Greek narratives, the gods interrupt normal causality and make any strictly human truth-seeking effort futile. But Foucault states that in Oedipus (in contrast to Homer), while the gods and the oracles can make nature produce signs at will – signs that are not the effects of natural causes (e.g. Zeus' thunderbolt) – even these supernatural signs require a protracted process of interpretation and clue-following that is not itself supernatural.

The Sherlock-like dimension of Oedipus' quest is, Foucault says, a 'techne', an art or craft:

> Oedipus's *techne* is this art of discovery that uses signs, traces, and marks, that allows us to go from what we don't know to what we do know by piecing together material elements that lead from one to the other.
>
> (Foucault 2014: 75)

In this way, what we could call 'forensic truth' is born. This is a truth that refers to an event in the past, but must be recounted in the present in order to re-establish order and deliver justice. It is a factual, not abstract or normative truth. And it is a truth that is never immediately apparent, but must be pieced together retrospectively by interrogating witnesses and scrutinizing 'traces and marks', that is, clues. Finally, forensic truth is a truth that, ideally, is acknowledged by the wrongdoer him/herself – whether the avowal is spontaneous and ethically driven or whether it is somewhat coerced, as in the case of the patient Leuret or, to give a non-Foucaultian example, Hercule Poirot's cornered criminals.

In the character of Oedipus, as interpreted by Foucault, we thus have a one-man modern criminal justice system. He begins the investigation, he interprets clues, he then seeks out witnesses and subjects their evidence to the scrutiny of the chorus/jury; and, in the end – after the chorus has found him guilty – he passes sentence on himself and punishes himself by putting out his eyes. And all the elements of this one-man criminal justice system can be shown to have later been borrowed, purposively or accidentally, by all manner of other knowledge enterprises.

Among all the elements or aspects of the justice process that are brought together in and by Oedipus, some are of more interest to Foucault than others. The punishment function, for example, while central to *Discipline and Punish*, remains of marginal interest in the lectures discussed here. And what I call the detective or forensic function is similarly of little interest to Foucault. Instead, the Louvain lectures that follow the long discussion of Greek sources focus on two things: 1) the history of avowal, from the Stoics to medieval monastic practices of penance; 2) the history of various mechanisms for presenting factual truths in court and weighing the evidence.

The first of these topics is developed through a close reading of numerous ethical and religious texts, and so it is less directly relevant to criminology. The rest of this chapter will thus focus instead on the last three Rio lectures and the final two lectures in Louvain, in a synthetic manner.

Tests, ordeals and the rebirth of the inquiry: the origins of modern justice

In pursuing the later history, in Western Europe, of courtroom mechanisms for establishing truth in the pursuit of justice, Foucault focuses on the fact that the mode of truth-seeking and truth-certification pioneered in the Greek tragedy (which he calls 'inquiry') was for a considerable time set aside or forgotten, displaced by the emergence of a kind of agonistic mechanism – the test. In the early Middle Ages, Foucault notes, jousts between knights reprised in a different context the dynamics of Homer's chariot race. Germanic justice too relied on quasi-Homeric tests (Foucault 2000: 36). Similarly, the tests and ordeals that were used to discover whether someone was indeed a witch relied neither on the factual evidence of witnesses nor on the impartial and rational judgement of a jury, but rather on the much older idea that God would reveal the truth by means of physical signs, as the gods and oracles of the ancient Greeks once did. Some legal techniques existed to settle disputes – anticipating modern tort law, one could add – but criminal prosecutions did not use the investigative and truth-testing techniques foreshadowed in *Oedipus Rex*.

But later in the Middle Ages there was in Europe a 'second birth of the inquiry' (Foucault 2000: 34). Fights and ordeals and private dispute resolution mechanisms were marginalized in quasi-legal and legal contexts by the rediscovery of techniques of truth involving the patient collection of factual information and the assessment of that information by a collective or a singular authority. And, as in ancient Greece, legal mechanisms and legal quests for truth played a key role in the history of truth technologies. Indeed, legal and quasi-legal investigations were 'the mold, the model on the basis of which a series of other knowledges – philosophical, rhetorical and empirical– were able to develop' (Foucault 2000: 34). While in Greek society the progress of the inquiry 'remained stationary',[4] in the late Middle Ages the inquiry 'would acquire extraordinary dimensions. Its destiny would be practically coextensive with the particular destiny of so-called "European" or "Western" culture' (ibid.).

In the Rio lectures – but not in Louvain– Foucault makes a point of connecting the evolution of legal truth mechanisms to broader institutional trends, in particular the rise of centralized, royal courts of justice and the emergence of a figure 'without precedent in Roman law – the prosecutor' (Foucault 2000: 42). The old notion of seeking out factual information by interrogating witnesses and scrutinizing clues (the traces in the present of past wrongs) was now deployed to help strengthen a new machinery of law, namely that of state criminal justice. Wrongs committed against other people now became crimes against the sovereign and/or the state, and the pursuit of the truth about crime and criminals now became a function of the central state. But the story of modern criminal justice is but one of the multifarious heirs of the ancient Greek experiments in inquiry.

The inquisitorial roots of modern science

Alongside the rise of royal courts of justice, Europe also witnessed a process by which Church authorities developed sophisticated methods of inquiry to root out heresy and witchcraft, and certify who had actually converted to Christianity and who was either a heretic or an impostor. Indeed, Foucault even claims that the inquiry, in its late medieval form, was more highly developed within the Church than anywhere else, and was only borrowed by legal state authorities from the Church, particularly the Inquisition.

Once relocated within the state, the inquiry, as a mode of gathering and certifying knowledge, was used not only in criminal law contexts but also for other purposes: to establish the wealth of a kingdom, for example. Censuses, land surveys and other mechanisms of state power/knowledge were important offshoots in the history of the inquiry. And state authorities did not monopolize the inquiry: explorers and scientists too developed techniques for subjecting the earth itself to inquiries (Foucault 2000: 48–50).

In the seventeenth and eighteenth centuries, inquiries proliferated. Under that name, European intellectuals pursued any number of investigations: some concerned the health and wealth of populations; some were philosophical inquiries into human understanding; and some speculated on the origin of language or the origin of human inequality, often using 'inquiry' in the title or the subtitle of their works.

Frustratingly, neither the Rio lectures nor the Louvain lectures provide explicit links to Foucault's work on biopolitics and governmentality, which obviously converges with the genealogy of the inquiry. This omission is understandable given that even in 1981 (when the Louvain lectures were given) most of that work remained unpublished, and so Foucault could hardly cross-reference his own work or expect his audience to be familiar with its terms. But what can we, with the wealth of posthumous publications we have, now say about the relation between the genealogy of truth-telling, avowal and inquiry that was presented in Rio and in Louvain and the posthumously published work on biopolitics and governmentality that has been so hugely influential?

The key point, in my view, is that, unlike in most of his other work on the genealogy of modern knowledges, in these Rio and Louvain lectures Foucault gives pride of place to legal and proto-legal procedures and mechanisms. It was in judicial and legal contexts, we are told, that Europe refined different forms of 'inquiry' – with the inquiry, to repeat, being described as that form of knowledge production whose 'destiny would be practically coextensive with the particular destiny of so-called "European" or "Western" culture' (Foucault 2000: 34).

But what about the 'avowal', that technique of self that is also a technique of truth – that form, taken to extremes by Christian theologians from the Reformation onward, that had developed as early as classical Greek tragedy? Did the rise of the inquiry, which over time became an objectivist, more or less positivistic and often top-down enterprise, marginalize the more intersubjective and embodied practices of acknowledging and telling the truth that Foucault studied in his work on ethics and subjectivity (Foucault 1997)?

The issue of how forms of avowal developed with or against forms of inquiry is not explicitly answered by Foucault, mainly because in the Louvain lectures the discussion of the inquiry is very brief, and in the Rio lectures, where more is said about the inquiry, the avowal plays a minor role. But the last of the Louvain lectures provides a sweeping overview of the rise of objectivist criminology and psychiatry in the late nineteenth century that indirectly answers these questions.

The survival of 'avowal' in criminal law – and glimmers of a return to avowal in contemporary science

With the positivist criminology pioneered in the 1880s and 1890s, Foucault tells the Louvain criminologists, attention turned to objectively measuring the risk posed to society by offenders and dangerous people generally (Foucault 2014: 224); subjectivity now had little or no interest. These criminologists, just like their medical contemporaries (the pre-Freudian experts in mental medicine), believed that they could determine the truth about people and their wrongdoing merely by scrutinizing 'bad' people's bodies and souls. Therefore, no confession or other form of avowal was necessary. However, the criminal law, by contrast with criminology, continued to believe that taking responsibility is important. Therefore, forms of avowal were – and are – valued, especially for purposes of sentencing. But the sciences of madness and of crime, as distinct from law, stopped speaking with and to the accused, being almost wholly concerned with objectively establishing the risks to society and taking preventive measures.

The practice of avowal, which Foucault sees as a central if not the central piece of the penal institutions (Foucault 2014: 210), one that well after its medieval form had disappeared, eighteenth-century social contract theory revived (ibid.: 207), was thus marginalized from science – though it remained and still remains central to the criminal law. Scientific inquiries into individual pathology or into collective dysfunction were now monopolized by experts who, unlike Oedipus, were not interested in personal truths about offenders, the kinds of truths that are today largely passed on to prison chaplains, volunteer prison visitors and lower-level social workers, as well as parole boards. Perhaps more importantly – though Foucault does not go on to draw this conclusion – the scientific experts who from the late nineteenth century onward instituted inquiries into the causes of deviance and crime did not acknowledge their own wrongdoings or deviant identities. Not being interested in the subjectivity of individual offenders because of their focus on medicalized, objectivized deviant identities, aggregate figures and risk factors, they also lost the opportunity to work on their own selves. Unlike Oedipus, they never positioned themselves as wrongdoers as well as truth-seekers. In this way the close connection between forms of subjectivity and forms of truth-seeking and truth-certification that one sees not only in Oedipus but also throughout the long history of practices of embodied, situational truth-telling was lost.

In contemporary correctional administration, in such practices as classifying offenders according to risk of recidivism or risk of escape, knowledge is imagined and used as a one-way street in which a detached official or expert studies and classifies the subjectivity, the desires and the intentions of offenders, who are consistently treated as objects of analysis, not as interlocutors. The lesson of Oedipus (that king and criminal, law-maker and law-breaker, investigator and suspect might be identities that are not always mutually exclusive) is swept under the rug.

If administrative criminology has failed to recognize that everyone (including law-makers, prison psychologists and prison guards) has subjectivities and desires, there are by contrast other forms of knowledge – from feminist psychotherapy to innovative, peer-based addiction recovery strategies – that do see the relation between truth-telling and wrongdoing differently from old-fashioned positivist criminology and psychiatry. For that matter, there are forms of contemporary philosophy (within existentialist and phenomenological traditions) that also bring the subjectivity of the philosopher him/herself back in, thus reconnecting contemporary philosophy to the genealogy of avowal and enriching the array of available forms of truth-telling. Perhaps future scholars will go on to use Foucault's work on truth-telling to explore innovative ways of bringing the subjectivities of those who govern offenders and suspects (and those who make the laws) back into the frame.

Conclusion

In all his lectures on truth-telling – the ones in Berkeley in 1983 (Foucault 2001) as well as the Rio and Louvain lectures covered here – Foucault emphasizes that one very important role played by truth-telling practices is to speak truth to power, a social practice that has little in common with the scientific quest for objective truth. Speaking truth to power is nevertheless important amongst critical race analysts, feminists, prisoner advocates and many others who have as much or more to say about contemporary practices of punishment as mainstream criminology. To pursue the analysis of the inquiry and the avowal in a contemporary setting, therefore, will require scholars to be sensitive to recent developments. Far too many of Foucault's readers have imagined that whatever he said about Bentham's panopticon perfectly explains practices of surveillance today, without doing the hard work necessary to adapt Foucault's analysis and modify his tools as necessary.

In particular, avowal is practised today largely in pop-culture contexts such as TV talk shows, or in the lower reaches of criminal justice (in sentencing, probation and parole); but even if it is rarely glimpsed in high-status knowledge enterprises and venues, avowal has by no means been wholly replaced by objectivism. While official truths about wrongdoing and about deviance are largely scientific and objectivist (focusing, these days, on neurons, brain chemicals and risk scales rather than on Lombroso-era phrenology and physiognomy), the same people who are exposed to and governed by science are often also governed (and govern themselves) by all manner of frankly anti-scientific truth projects, from Alcoholics Anonymous to astrology. And some of these at least are indeed intersubjective and embodied – which makes Foucault's work on embodied truth-telling particularly relevant.

It is important nevertheless to note that mapping the complex and unexpected combinations of techniques of self and techniques of truth that have arisen in the very recent past was not Foucault's own project. Indeed, in all his lecture series, whether at the Collège de France or elsewhere, Foucault showed a marked reluctance to even hint at how our immediate present might be throwing up combinations of techniques of truth and techniques of self that differ from those established at the height of the disciplinary era. He often apologized to his audience for getting lost in the details of medieval monasticism or ancient Greek texts, and repeatedly claimed that he had simply run out of time and could not bring the story to the present. Such claims, however, now look rather disingenuous (given that we now have access to the text of a huge variety of very well-organized and carefully prepared lectures). Foucault wrote out almost every word of his lectures in advance, and often rewrote answers given in interviews before they were published. It is therefore unlikely that in heat of the moment he got carried away by his own spoken word and forgot to look at the lecture hall clock. So what explains his reticence to diagnose the present in his formal lectures and in his published writings, leaving his political comments to interviews?

The repeated comment about having spent so much time on historical and textual details that he 'ran out of time' to get to the present could be read, I suggest, as quietly signalling a particular practice of self. *Discipline and Punish*, for example, does not take us into the twentieth century, an authorial choice whose significance few readers consider; and in the case of a properly published book, one cannot say that one just ran out of time to get to the present. In my view, Foucault's choice to stop many of his most important analyses well before his own present indicates that he came up with quiet ways of strongly signalling that he did not want his work to be read as a new theory of modernity. His objective was rather to research and write genealogies of practices of power/knowledge with much contemporary relevance, but leaving it to his listeners and readers to make their own connections between his research and their observations about their particular contemporary context. The Rio lectures and the Louvain lectures are thus not a 'theory' of law's knowledge production to be verified by means of piles of examples, but, like Foucault's other works, always tentative, partial accounts of particular aspects of the history of the relations between truth, power and subjectivity.

Notes

1 While the term 'truth-telling' (from *dire-vrai* in French, which in turn, Foucault tells us, is meant to evoke Nietzsche's *Wahrsagen*) is found in many other English translations of Foucault's posthumously published lectures, the term *aveu* was mainly developed in the Louvain lectures. For that reason, it is extremely helpful that Harcourt and Brion provide a lengthy explanation of how the range of meanings of *aveu* is not coterminous with 'confession', the English term most commonly used by Foucault translators thus far when translating Foucault's brief comments on *aveu* found elsewhere (Foucault 2014). It should be noted, however, that Graham Burchell, like Harcourt and Brion a careful translator, includes the word *aveu* in parentheses where Foucault used *aveu* and not the French *confession* (Foucault 2010: 136).

2 I choose the word 'enlightened' advisedly. For the Collège de France 1982–83 course of lectures (Foucault 2010), where Foucault reprised a significant part of the previous year's Louvain lectures, Foucault chose to begin not with a psychiatrist forcing a patient to avow his illness, as in Louvain (Foucault 2014), but rather with a long and rather positive reflection on Kant's 'What is Enlightenment?' essay, a lecture that refutes the usual classification of Foucault as a 'postmodernist'. Not published until just after Foucault's death, the reflection on Kant's approach to Enlightenment, history and ethics was used by Habermas (1986), in a move of extreme bad taste, to claim that Foucault had finally given up on postmodernism in a sort of deathbed conversion to the goals of the liberal Enlightenment.

3 By contrast, Max Weber, who could not understand the not always rational epistemology of the common law, compares the modern common law jury not to the Greek chorus but to none other than the Greek oracle: 'the jury, as it were, thus took the place of the oracle, and indeed it resembles it inasmuch as it does not indicate a rational ground for its decision' (Weber 1968: 762). I would say that the reason juries give no reasons for their decision is not that they use oracular intuition but because their role is not to discover the truth step by step as scientists or good detectives do, but rather to make a global judgement about whose story is most truthful, based in part on their view of the 'character' of witnesses, not just the objective rationality of their statements. Juries consider truth claims in embodied form: hence the persistence of the jury, a mystery to Weber, can be understood with Foucault's tools, which link practices of self and embodiment to truth-telling and truth-certifying practices.

4 Whether Aristotle's work constitutes an example of what Foucault calls 'inquiry' or a departure from it is an interesting question that Foucault does not directly address. Aristotle certainly cultivated rigorous intellectual habits involving questioning both received truths and nature itself in a vaguely proto-Baconian manner; and he of course placed truth within the human, not the divine, realm. These points coincide with 'the inquiry'. However, his work, like philosophy more generally, appears – at least to us, who have access only to texts, not the social process by which they were produced – as monological. The intersubjective dynamics that are crucial in such endeavours as the investigation of crimes and the leading of witnesses do not appear in philosophical texts.

Bibliography

Foucault, Michel. 1976. *The History of Sexuality, Vol. I: An Introduction.* Translated by Robert Hurley. New York: Vintage.

Foucault, Michel. 1977. *Discipline and Punish: The Birth of the Prison*. Translated by Alan Sheridan. New York: Vintage.

Foucault, Michel. 1984. *The History of Sexuality, Vol. II: The Use of Pleasure*. Translated by Robert Hurley. New York: Vintage.

Foucault, Michel. 1988. *The History of Sexuality, Vol. III: The Care of the Self*. Translated by Robert Hurley. New York: Vintage.

Foucault, Michel. 1997. *Ethics: Subjectivity and Truth: Essential Works of Michel Foucault, 1954–1984, Vol. I*. Edited by Paul Rabinow. Translated by Robert Hurley. New York: New Press.

Foucault, Michel. 2000. *Power: Essential Works of Foucault, 1954–1984, Vol. III*. Edited by James D. Faubion. Translated by Robert Hurley. New York: New Press.

Foucault, Michel. 2001. *Fearless Speech*. Edited by Joseph Pearson. Los Angeles, CA: Semiotext(e).

Foucault, Michel. 2003. *'Society Must Be Defended': Lectures at the Collège de France, 1975–1976*. Translated by David Macey. New York: Picador.

Foucault, Michel. 2007. *Security, Territory, Population: Lectures at the Collège de France, 1977–1978*. Edited by Michel Senellart. Translated by Graham Burchell. New York: Picador/Palgrave Macmillan.

Foucault, Michel. 2010. *The Government of Self and Others: Lectures at the Collège de France, 1982–83*. Edited by Arnold I. Davidson. Translated by Graham Burchell. New York: Picador.

Foucault, Michel. 2014. *Wrong-Doing, Truth-Telling: The Function of Avowal in Justice*. Edited by Fabienne Brion and Bernard E. Harcourt. Translated by Stephen W. Sawyer. Chicago, IL: University of Chicago Press.

Foucault, Michel. 2015. *The Punitive Society: Lectures at the Collège de France 1972–1973*. Edited by Bernard E. Harcourt. Translated by Graham Burchell. Basingstoke: Palgrave Macmillan.

Habermas, Jurgen. 1986. 'Taking Aim at the Heart of the Present,' in David Couzens Hoy, ed., *Foucault: A Critical Reader*. Oxford: Blackwell, pp. 103–109.

Weber, Max. 1968. *Economy and Society: An Outline of Interpretive Sociology, Vol. II*. New York: Bedminster.

Chapter 8

Final reflections

Throughout this book I have tried to do a number of things that attentive readers may already have noticed are not necessarily in perfect harmony with one another. First, I have explained a good number of Foucault's key terms and ideas. Second, I have emphasized that Foucault's work is not a system made up of neatly organized concepts with static definitions: it is better characterized as a style of analysis. Let me first discuss the first and second goals and the tension between them, before adding some final, largely methodological comments.

If Foucault himself kept turning his own ideas over to reveal new facets, unearth unknown genealogies, discover new meanings, find unexpected uses for techniques of governance previously thought to belong to one system, and thus enable innovative analytical possibilities, it stands to reason that it would be inappropriate to treat his work as if it were a system. General timeless claims – for example, the nineteenth-century belief that social evolution is unidirectional and that Western European societies, with their complex division of labour, are more evolved and thus superior to other societies – are not so much refuted by Foucault as sidelined. Quite simply, his work does not proceed by generating fixed truth claims and grand theories about human history. Thus, all of the explanations and quasi-definitions of Foucault's terms that I have provided (and I had to provide them in keeping with the first, textbook-like goal) have to be taken by the reader with a grain of salt, given the fact that Foucault himself emphasized the historical specificity of his discoveries and insights.

In this book it has been my aim not only to explain Foucault's ideas but also to give occasional practical demonstrations of how one might think in a Foucaultian manner about both the present and the past. Other careful readers of Foucault might well disagree with some of my examples and creative applications. It is important to note that it is Foucault's own approach that is responsible for the fact that I cannot claim the kind of authority that textbook writers generally assume. Readers who consult other secondary sources, or who are brave enough to read Foucault's texts for themselves, are not here exhorted to treat my explanations as the one source of real authority. If there is no ultimate truth in the human sciences, as Foucault famously believed – but only contextually specific and always revisable truths about certain games of truth, power, subjectivity and knowledge that are played across a wide array of institutions – so too there is not going to be any ultimate truth in Foucault interpretation.

But, as Foucault himself would have said, just because there is no absolute truth does not mean that we cannot get on with research and generate new insights. It is only those who expect truths to be timeless who then disappointedly sink into relativism upon discovering that there can be no absolute truth in human sciences. Those who take up more pragmatist and/or more historically grounded approaches will not be particularly disturbed to see disagreements amongst well-informed people, since in most cases the disagreements arise because they are not really speaking about the same situation or entity (even if they use the same word). Thus, throughout the book I have tried to provide some original examples, mainly from our contemporary world, that demonstrate the continuing relevance of work that was done by Foucault decades ago and that, for the most part, use sources that were already centuries old. In Chapter 7, for example, I gestured toward the relevance of Foucault's analysis of 'avowal' to understanding the 'personal truth games' that fascinate audiences every day in police procedurals, true-crime narratives and reality-TV shows. This book is not the place to carry out a Foucaultian analysis of contemporary popular culture; but it is my hope that some of this book's readers will pick up the baton and pursue such concrete analyses of the games of truth and games of power that we can see every day both in real-life criminal justice settings and in popular representations of crime and justice.

This brings us to the question of using Foucault's work for criminology. It was mentioned in the introductory chapter that while modern criminal law scholarship and teaching has focused on *acts* (what is in fact criminalized and what is not; what acts should be criminalized), criminology has instead chosen to focus on two other types of object of study. One is *persons*, taken either individually (as in criminological psychology) or in groups (as in the sociology of deviance and in studies of community social cohesion and social disorder). The other common object of criminological study consists of *institutions*, mainly institutions of criminal justice but now often also including others – from private security firms to community agencies to spy agencies to private corporations such as Google or Facebook. Clearly, notions such as 'normalization' or terms such as 'biopolitics' can help shed light on the less obvious and less directly coercive forms of power that are exercised both over individuals and over particular groups by various actors and institutions using specialized knowledges (such as statistics, CCTV camera footage or Internet data mining). Plenty of available studies show how Foucault's work can be fruitfully used to develop criminology. But, in emphasizing that techniques initially associated with one institution (the prison, the police department) quickly travel to other spheres and may indeed flourish elsewhere, Foucault's method tends to undermine the existence of specialities such as 'prison scholarship', 'policing scholarship' and so on; and, more importantly, it casts some doubt on the autonomy of 'criminology'.

Foucault's approach to studying powers and knowledges can certainly help us to further criminological research, as has been amply proven by the burgeoning Foucaultian criminology literature; but, taken as a whole, his work simultaneously puts in question the assumptions that underpin the whole criminological enterprise – specifically, the assumption that the business of criminal law and criminology is to study and classify *acts, persons, and/or institutions*. If this book had a subtitle it would be 'Foucault for – and against– criminology'.

I will take the three key traditional objects of criminal law and criminological study (acts, persons, institutions) in turn, and proceed to raise some (largely unanswerable) questions that draw on Foucault's general approach.

Why does the criminal law focus on willed acts?

In relation to acts (which in this context means not acts of God or of nature but rather the humanly 'willed' acts that may or may not fall under the jurisdiction of criminal law), it should be abundantly clear that reading Foucault does not help at all with the normative questions about whether act X or Y should or should not be criminalized. However, reading Foucault's work can help a great deal towards putting the rise of criminal law thought and criminal law scholarship in perspective and raise some fundamental questions about both the 'actus' of *actus reus* and the 'mens' of *mens rea*. In doing so it can help us stand back from the endless debates about which acts should not be included in criminal codes, and instead ask the perhaps unanswerable question of why it might be that generations of both practitioners (from detectives to judges) and criminal law professors have been obsessed with governing willed acts and understanding the social world in terms of 'acts'.

As seen in Chapters 6 and 7, Foucault's research on the history of 'truth-telling' practices highlighted the curious fascination that Western religious, psychiatric and legal authorities have shown with the question of telling the truth about one's self, especially the wrongs that one has done. Why has Western culture insisted, throughout the centuries and across a variety of institutions, that among the many harms that occur, acts that are willed by individual humans should be singled out for particular scrutiny and, potentially, grave punishment? This may sound like the kind of idle question that interests only philosophers, but it has major practical implications. Here we can just mention the fact that the deliberately planned murder of a single person usually draws a much heavier punishment than the death of many people in floods or fires caused by global climate change. Climate change is arguably 'willed', by commission as well as omission; but it is not willed in classic *mens rea* manner by an identifiable set of particular individuals whose acts are limited to a particular locale and whose conscious goal is to cause harm.

The penal law's obsession with consciously planned acts willed by identifiable individuals is accompanied (in Western cultures, not necessarily in other contexts) by a quasi-religious obsession with 'avowal'. From early Christianity to today's criminal trials, it has been widely assumed that those who do wrong must also avow their wrongdoing (or, after the rise of discipline, must avow a deviant identity that ultimately caused them to commit those acts). Wrongdoers are supposed to more or less publicly admit that they both committed certain acts and that they willed the acts in question. Foucault does not give a general 'theory' to explain this phenomenon, and in his lectures and other writings he emphasizes that various practices of avowal and truth-telling have served different purposes at different times and in different institutional contexts. But one gathers that Foucault is trying to make a very familiar set of assumptions strange by showing how downright bizarre and even ridiculous the quest to make wrongdoers avow their sins or their deviant nature can become – as in the example, mentioned in Chapter 7, of the psychiatrist who repeatedly subjected a patient to ice-cold showers to force him to admit that the visions he had were products of his diseased mind.

Foucault's work on avowal, when combined with his very different work on the disciplinary techniques used in correctional institutions, can help us take a step back and put in question authorities' obsession with enlisting the very person who is accused of doing or being something undesirable in the process of establishing the official truth. Why should it matter so much if an accused person refuses to admit personal responsibility? Why is maintaining silence and not testifying at one's trial often taken as a sign of guilt? Why is there such a close relation – an assumed relation – between sincerity or authenticity on the one hand and eligibility for mercy or for parole on the other? And why should criminal justice, and the criminal trial in particular, be such an important arena in which these games of personal as well as factual truth are played out? If I sue a contractor or if I fail to pay a parking ticket, those legal events are unlikely to become the fodder for major public debates where perfect strangers discuss and evaluate my overall worthiness as a human being. But the criminal process provides a constant stream of opportunities for general discussions about factual truth, personal worthiness, authenticity, guilt, responsibility and, last but not least, the nature of good and evil.

Thus, Foucault's work is not at all interested in or useful for debating questions such as 'should the *act* of providing an abortion be criminalized?' What it can do instead is help us critically question the peculiarly Western fascination with inquiries into acts – willed acts – which then tend to become inquiries into the deep self and hidden desires of the person (the type of person) who is accused of committing the acts. In relation to the criminalization of abortion, Foucault would encourage us to ask: why and how did abortion get criminalized in the first place? What was being governed through this criminalization? How were competing knowledges deployed to legalize abortion? And so on.

Persons: individuals, normalization, identity

If the criminal law has traditionally dealt in 'acts', criminology developed in large part as an inquiry not so much into particular acts as into persons. Now, Foucault famously argued that sexuality is a very important if not the most important site for the elaboration of modern truths about persons. (Sex has of course always existed, but 'sexuality' is a modern invention.) Personal facts such as one's ethnicity and religion and profession certainly matter both to people themselves and to those around them; but sexuality is a particularly important site both for scrutiny by authorities and peers and for self-discovery. The modern 'gay' identity is the best exemplar here; but Foucault's analysis also lends itself to understanding the emergence of other identities, from 'sexual psychopath' to 'sex addict' to 'heterosexual'.

What does this have to say to criminology today? One thing it could say is that, when observing the rapid proliferation of very coercive rules and laws governing the new and expansive category of 'sex offender', Foucault would incite us to ask questions such as 'Why is it that sexual offences are regarded as worse and as more indicative of a deep and indelible character flaw than other offences?'; and 'When and how did sexuality turn into a site of major victimization and unavoidable trauma, when as recently as the 1970s the erotic realm was regarded by many women as well as men as a key site of freedom and pleasurable desire?'

Sexuality is an excellent arena in which to discern the relevance of Foucault's argument, made in *Discipline and Punish* (1977) as well as in many other places, that the same governing processes that produce groups such as the normal and the deviant, the 'gifted' and the deficient, the disciplined and the undisciplined also produce modern individuality itself. How do we become individuals? Paradoxically, we become individuals by being subject to 'normalization'. Doing well in maths or doing badly in reading become for children indicators of who they are as unique individuals. Parents routinely normalize their children in this manner, repeating to visitors that child X is good with people and child Y is a bookworm, thus placing them on specific spots along various normal curves, in ways that then become internalized and help shape their own sense of self. Our sense of individuality is thus paradoxically produced largely by adding a series of normalizing judgements and formal or informal test results – that is how Western individuals define themselves as 'unique'.

The point for legal studies is that the legal person who is held responsible for certain acts defined as criminal (or as insane or otherwise abnormal) has not always been an individual with a deep but knowable psychic identity. Non-Western legal systems certainly define some people (persons) as criminals, as did premodern Western legal systems; but only Western modernity came to govern madness, crime, sexuality and other issues on the basis of the unspoken assumption that acts that are wrong or just unusual are often rooted in or are symptoms of some kind of deep inner identity that the psy-sciences can uncover and measure. This identity is regarded (including by the people concerned) as their 'individuality'. Thus, Foucault shows that the same governing processes that give us building blocks that we use to construct and govern our own individual identity also create 'normal' distributions, means, standard deviations, averages and every known technique for standardizing human conduct and human desires.

Having given some sense of how Foucault's work can help criminological research become more aware of its own assumptions about 'acts', about the persons who commit acts, and about individuality and identity, we now move to the third dimension of criminology – that is the institutional scale. As mentioned in Chapter 1, the rise of critical criminology in the 1960s and 1970s was associated with a shift away from the study of criminals and crime and towards the study of the institutions that not only govern crime and criminals but that also produce these entities, by stigmatization and other techniques. Foucault was certainly interested in furthering the critical study of institutions, criminal justice ones included; but, as we shall see, his approach encourages us to avoid taking particular institutions (or even criminal justice as a whole) as if they were self-contained. Let us now see what that would mean for criminology.

De-centring institutions

As discussed briefly in Chapter 1, Foucault parted company with the symbolic interactionist and other critical studies of mental health and criminal justice institutions by making an important methodological move – namely, focusing on how particular practices for governing people, populations and spaces were borrowed across institutions. This connects with the comments in Chapter 2 about why Foucault's *Discipline and Punish* is not a history of the prison, as is often assumed, but rather a study of 'the birth of the prison' that shows that the classic penitentiaries of the nineteenth century did not invent most of their techniques (cells, uniforms, schedules, silent labour, etc.), but rather borrowed the techniques from earlier, mostly religious or military institutions. In turn, techniques developed for purposes of governing prisoners (such as the panopticon) were quickly adapted for use in all manner of other contexts. Foucault, it is important to repeat, was not a criminologist; studying the rise of the penitentiary was not an end in itself but only a means to an end. The end was to understand the origins of a particular subset of the multiple techniques that are used in contemporary societies to govern individuals, populations and spaces.

Studying the history of imprisonment from a non-criminological or even anti-criminological point of view meant that Foucault was able to emphasize the linkages between apparently separate legal and criminological topics better than most criminologists. That a close reading of Homeric epics might shed some light on how justice was determined before there were judges, juries and even witnesses – thus helping us to not take our current legal practices for granted (as described in Chapter 7) – could only happen because Foucault did not set out to contribute to any particular discipline or field of study. He pursued the study of practices of governance, practices of truth-telling and practices for governing oneself wherever the path might lead. If along that path he realized he had to delve into dusty tomes classified as 'political economy', as 'theology' or as 'psychiatry', then so be it.

It is very doubtful that in today's highly 'disciplined' academy – where knowledge is imparted to students (or is published in journals) only after being previously and quietly sorted into 'disciplines' and 'fields' that present themselves as if they have always existed – a figure like Foucault could prosper. One can only imagine what a criminology journal would have said if Foucault submitted a chapter of *Discipline and Punish* for publication: 'an amateur piece, the author has ignored all the relevant literature.' Today, books can sometimes push against disciplinarization, but journal articles are rigidly disciplined (including by those in control of journals in interdisciplinary fields); and, when teaching courses, it is very difficult to break with the basic expectations that students as well as administrators have about what a criminology course or a law course could include. At the Collège de France professors can call their courses anything they like, but everywhere else one must work within a pre-made discipline or interdisciplinary field. A cross-departmental course in the history of knowledge practices and knowledge formats could perhaps exist; but in virtually all institutions such a course could exist only within a particular department (e.g. anthropology) or across two such departments, and would have to draw primarily on one or two set traditions.

Today criminology has become not only largely separate from cognate fields such as criminal law and social history, but has also become highly specialized and fragmented by methods used and theorists referenced as well as by substantive field. Authors who submit articles to journals are thus disciplined before they even submit their paper. At most they can make the claim that to study problem X, the bread and butter of journal A, it would be useful to draw some ideas from research in field B. Recently, for example, some theoretical work in geography has been adapted for use by legal studies and criminology. But such a move still takes the fields as given, arguing only that content or research methods for that already established field could be taken from a new source. To that extent, books that explain Foucault while remaining true to his spirit would all have to be entitled 'Foucault for and against policing studies', 'Foucault for and against anthropology', 'Foucault for and against geography', etc.

Thus, while it is true that Foucault's work is being used by researchers in many fields to uncover the constant and unpredictable 'translations' by which practices and techniques are borrowed across institutions, the Foucaultian methodological focus on practices and techniques necessarily has the effect of de-centring the institutions that have given rise to well-defined bodies of scholarship, including criminological scholarship. Foucault's work reminds us that institutions such as prisons did not necessarily emerge from the mind of prison experts, but were rather pragmatic responses to problems that were not necessarily 'crime' problems – responses elaborated, usually in an ad hoc manner, by people with a variety of backgrounds and interests.

Similarly, many of the features of the modern criminal trial that we take for granted as essential to criminal justice turn out to have evolved without a definite plan, adapted from diverse sources at different times in a largely ad hoc manner. These features of the criminal trial reflect implicit ideas and ideals about truth-seeking; about the need to certify truth claims; and about moral responsibility that may not be properly understood if studied only within the rather narrow scope of the history of criminal law and criminal justice.

Finally, what one could call the forensic impulse or gaze – the desire to establish the truth of a particular crime or wrong so as to restore a social order that is understood as the default setting, as natural and normal – is a phenomenon that is hardly limited to the history of policing and detective work. Some criminologists might say, 'great, this means that I can remain a policing scholar but now go on to study all manner of truth-seeking exercises'. However, it would not be very plausible to assimilate the varied history of quasi-forensic investigative techniques and truth-certifying techniques into the established field of policing. For one thing, people who study psychiatric practice (among many other fields) could also claim that after reading Foucault they too have decided that all practices focused on the truths of the self belong to their particular enterprise. The current organization of academic knowledge thus makes it very difficult for anyone, student or professor, to follow in Foucault's footsteps. Using Foucault to reform or update either criminology in general or subfields such as punishment studies or policing studies is an inherently contradictory task, since sooner or later pursuing Foucaultian lines of inquiry will mean questioning the very field to which one wants to contribute.

At this point the 'normal' way for an author to proceed would be to find some reason – quite against this concluding chapter's run of play – to be optimistic about the future of criminology. Academic books as well as personal stories are supposed to end with a cheerful declaration of closure. 'The road ahead may be difficult but if we adopt X or Y remedy we can get out of the current swamp and renew the discipline/field' is the kind of conclusion that theory books as well as self-discovery narratives seem to call for. Readers who have travelled this far into the book will already know that any trite conclusion along these lines would be completely contrary to Foucault's spirit.

However, scepticism and historical research are not necessarily the only options for someone who takes Foucault seriously. It may be the case that some of the readers of this book feel up to the non-Foucaultian or post-Foucaultian task of imagining a revolutionary future for criminological research – a future that does not take acts, individuals, identities or institutions for granted, and that does not assume that criminal law and criminal justice are self-contained domains whose history can be understood internally. Those readers might perhaps be found in new fields that for their own reasons are also challenging some of modernity's key assumptions (such as the centrality of acts and persons).

One intellectual enterprise that, from a totally non-Foucaultian perspective, radically displaces and de-centres acts, persons and institutions is indigenous thought on justice and law. Indigenous philosophies do not privilege the individual and his/her free will, focusing instead on relationships, duties, processes, consequences and ecologies. And deploying virtually any indigenous knowledge will inevitably blur the boundaries separating one institution from another, most strikingly in the case of law, which as far as I know is not regarded in indigenous contexts as a distinct institution or a separate body of thought with its own officials and experts. Indigenous thinkers are unlikely to be interested in many of Foucault's analyses, unless they have their own reasons for critically engaging with the history of Western governance. But perhaps scholars who are younger and less European than I (especially in Australia, New Zealand and Canada, where there is a great resurgence of indigenous legal thought) may begin to synthesize or juxtapose Foucault's critical analysis of the historical emergence of the 'free individual' with indigenous perspectives about justice – perspectives that necessarily de-centre not only the modern individual but even human beings, who are generally considered as but one type of natural entity.

Similarly, there may be some creative connections made in the future between Foucaultian analyses of modernity and environmental criminology. After all, the very idea of environmental criminology requires abandoning the traditional criminal law–criminology commitment to closely inquiring into individuals, their acts and their inner identities. Climate change is a disaster of unprecedented proportions since, unlike the wars of the past (and the present), it threatens not only one country or people or a few countries but the Earth itself. It may become apparent as climate change worsens that to face threats that exist at a truly global scale it is a little futile to continue focusing on individuals, their acts and their identities, and continuing to isolate one small set of institutions (those of criminal justice, say) for study, as if they were indeed a separate system. There may indeed be hitherto undiscovered connections between the admittedly dysfunctional institutions of criminal justice (prisons, especially, but perhaps also criminal trials) and the larger systems of equally dysfunctional governance that are blocking the timely application of the scientific and economic remedies that could be utilized to halt and reverse climate change.

So perhaps criminological research – especially research that draws from some of the new, post-Enlightenment and post-European frameworks that are emerging today – can survive its encounter with Foucault, and can even benefit from such an encounter. But only time will tell.

Bibliography

Foucault, Michel. 1977. *Discipline and Punish: The Birth of the Prison*. Translated by Alan Sheridan. New York: Vintage.

Index

Taylor & Francis eBooks

eBooks

from Taylor & Francis

Helping you to choose the right eBooks for your Library

Add to your library's digital collection today with Taylor & Francis eBooks. We have over 50,000 eBooks in the Humanities, Social Sciences, Behavioural Sciences, Built Environment and Law, from leading imprints, including Routledge, Focal Press and Psychology Press.

ORDER YOUR FREE INSTITUTIONAL TRIAL TODAY

Free Trials Available

We offer free trials to qualifying academic, corporate and government customers.

Choose from a range of subject packages or create your own!

Benefits for you

- Free MARC records
- COUNTER-compliant usage statistics
- Flexible purchase and pricing options
- 70% approx of our eBooks are now DRM-free.

Benefits for your user

- Off-site, anytime access via Athens or referring URL
- Print or copy pages or chapters
- Full content search
- Bookmark, highlight and annotate text
- Access to thousands of pages of quality research at the click of a button.

eCollections

Choose from 20 different subject eCollections, including:

- Asian Studies
- Economics
- Health Studies
- Law
- Middle East Studies

eFocus

We have 16 cutting-edge interdisciplinary collections, including:

- Development Studies
- The Environment
- Islam
- Korea
- Urban Studies

For more information, pricing enquiries or to order a free trial, please contact your local sales team:

UK/Rest of World: **online.sales@tandf.co.uk**
USA/Canada/Latin America: **e-reference@taylorandfrancis.com**
East/Southeast Asia: **martin.jack@tandf.com.sg**
India: **journalsales@tandfindia.com**

www.tandfebooks.com

For Product Safety Concerns and Information please contact our EU representative GPSR@taylorandfrancis.com Taylor & Francis Verlag GmbH, Kaufingerstraße 24, 80331 München, Germany